How To Turn 39

Colin Wright

Library of Congress Cataloging-In-Publication Data

How To Turn 39 / Colin Wright — 1st ed.
ISBN: 978-1-964123-00-4
eISBN: 978-1-964123-01-1

1. Aging. 2. Self-Help. 3. Essays. 4. Personal Growth.
5. Communication.

Cover design by Colin Wright.

For those who left us messages in bottles, and for those who will read the messages we leave.

Foreword

When I was in my late-teens, I assumed that at age 35 I would be at the height of my powers.

From that youthful perspective, my mid-thirties would grant me all the prominence and benefits of full-on adulthood—relationships, resources, respect—but few of the age-related issues that seem to become stumbling-blocks for folks past that point: health problems especially, but also midlife-crises, child-rearing responsibilities, financial burdens, and issues related to retirement.

As I write this, I'm 38-years-old and just a few weeks from my 39th birthday.

Neither age is important as we often measure such things, but having left 35 in the rearview (what feels like) lifetimes ago, I've spent a fair portion of the past several years thinking and learning about what it means to grow older, which I hope will be useful as I approach the (more culturally meaningful) age of 40.

I don't believe age has to be a barrier to growth and fulfillment, but I do believe how we think about aging determines how well we adjust to our changing bodies, minds, and lives.

At this moment in history, aging is inevitable: it's not something we can avoid or negotiate with. But that doesn't mean we can't do it with intent and some degree of control.

Despite its many downsides (and there are quite a few), I see aging as something we get to do, not something we're cursed to experience. What follows is a collection of thoughts on the subject, leaning toward how we might better traverse the chronological distance between "who I am now," and "who I believe I can become."

As with all my books, please graze broadly, keep an open mind, and take or discard whatever you choose: we're all different, and what makes sense to me might be nonsensical to you (and that's as it should be).

Let's jump in.

What Aging Is

Aging is a biological reality.

At its most basic, it refers to the breakdown of processes that otherwise keep our physical form repairing, recycling, regenerating, and otherwise ticking along in a productive (and reproductive) manner.

Some of our organs and systems, and thus some cells of which they consist, begin to go early: it varies, but we're prone to eye-muscle issues (leading to focusing problems) at around 35, we start losing body mass at around age 30, fertility in women peaks and then declines beginning in our late-20s, and as older teenagers we've already lost some of the hearing (especially in higher frequency ranges) we enjoyed as children.

Sunlight chemically ages our skin from day one, and the evidence of this deterioration becomes more apparent as the processes that previously repaired the afflicted skin cells start to surrender their youthful gusto.

Our hair grays, and a quarter to half of all people, both men and women, experience at least irregular hair loss by around age 50.

We become increasingly frail because of diminished musculature and connective tissue, weakened bones, and the breakdown of cartilage in our joints. Some of us become less mobile (which amplifies these issues) while others remain active but enjoy fewer benefits from our efforts than we would have in earlier years, at times triggering harmful biological outcomes instead of healthful ones.

Difficult to avoid environmental and lifestyle variables like our activity and stress levels, along with our dietary choices, compound genetic predispositions that can accelerate the hardening of vital vessels and the accumulation of plaque in our cardiovascular systems.

Many of these biotic burdens peak after our prime child-having years and kick into a higher gear around middle-age, when (it's suspected) our bodies don't really know what to do with themselves anymore and the maintenance systems that were functioning at a high level to keep us primed and ready to pass on our DNA to the next generation transition into something akin to senioritis: still ticking along, but with less enthusiasm and intention than before.

Aging is also a cultural and legal construct.

We're told that marking the years we're alive is meaningful, and we're told that various things happen—or should happen—when we're 18, 21, 40, and so on.

Because of a slew of age-related cultural understandings and norms, we imbue birthdays with near-magical significance, even if our biological realities (how we physically age) will be dissimilar to those of our age-demographic peers.

Rules and laws reinforce our age-related folkways by carving society into groups based on when we were born.

We can legally drink, are required to pay taxes, and may be sent to fight in military conflicts based on the chronological specifics of our births. While the physical and mental distinctions between people born a few days apart may be minor (on average, at least), those few days determine (in a legal sense) who is conscripted and who isn't, who gets segregated into which grade level at school, and who can drive a car (and who will be punished if they're caught doing so).

Research suggests many "oldest person in the world" records are probably the consequence of bad record-keeping and fraud: folks who seem to live well into their 100-teens are actually years or decades younger, the system either mis-designating them because of faulty or absent paperwork, or because they pretend to be older family members (like their parents) to receive financial support from their government.

Some "Blue Zones" where people ostensibly live longer than folks elsewhere around the world are seemingly also the consequence of flawed paperwork and governmental systems, not super-powered genes or cuisines or landscapes or climates that shape and sustain a profusion of regional Methuselahs.

Our perception of age can thus be guided by the tangible reality of what our brains and bodies do and what we go through because of those internal happenings, but this perception can also be significantly influenced by state structures and cultural assumptions about who we're meant to be and what we're meant to be doing during different age-bracketed eras.

Biological reality and governmental decree provide a scaffolding for age-related presumptions, then, but traditional notions about who does what at which age also give rise to permissions and limitations, and these inherited notions inform our personal ambitions and goals at discrete (often invented) life stages.

Wrangling the variables that shape our individual understandings of and assumptions about aging, then, is a multifaceted task that requires we attain an understanding of our physicalities and mentalities, but also that we develop a sense of our place within external structures, some of which we will consciously recognize and others that will be impalpable but fundamental to the formation of our collective and individual aging-related beliefs.

Purpose and Legacy

What are we doing, why, and to what end?

Are the decisions we make each day meaningful, or are we trying to imbue meaningless things with significance so as not to feel lost, alone, and rudderless as we traverse the tides and eddies of corporeal existence?

One way of thinking about meaning is that everything we do is meaningful because our actions (or inactions) bridge the gap between one state of being and another. I was sitting in a chair, now I'm standing, and that movement, my decision to stand and the subsequent act of standing moved my life and my body forward, making everything else I did for the rest of the day (and ultimately, the rest of my life) possible.

In this framing, meaning is just another way of thinking about causality and one thing leading to another. The future only happens because of what we do in the present, and things are only the way they are today because of what happened in the past.

We thus shape the future through every thought and act and outcome, and that suffuses the whole of our lives, even the seemingly insignificant stuff, with immense, reality-shaping importance.

Another way of thinking about meaning is through the lens of purpose.

If we can figure out why we exist, what we're meant to do and not do, there's a much clearer line connecting what we do and the outcomes to which we contribute.

Some of us look to spirituality and faith to gain insight into our personal purpose, others discover and cultivate purpose via more worldly means.

I believe, for instance, that there are an endless number of ways we might live purposefully, every one of us capable of intentionally shaping ourselves and the world, and consequently playing an active role in how everything turns out.

Our existence is a variable in the grand scheme of things, so we'll influence things no matter what. But to do things a particular way, and to know why we do the things we do, adds directionality to our lives so that we act with agency, rather than behaving like leaves in the wind: moving, but without conscious guidance or purpose.

From this perspective, then, meaning is about motivated action and impact (that motivation shaped by our beliefs, knowledge, and experience), rather than a detached, unconscious locomotion.

Many of us find meaning in the idea of legacy; of perpetuating something of ourselves so that our finite physicality doesn't prevent us from achieving a sort of immortality.

The pursuit of this type of meaning might manifest as donations to charities, the construction of buildings, bridges, and other works that our fellow humans will use well into the future, or even historic accomplishments like curing a disease or discovering a new star.

Many of us establish legacy through our children, passing on our genes and our beliefs to the next generation, in this way perpetuating something of ourselves, even though we won't, personally, be around as long as our genetic and intellectual lineage.

We might categorize this type of meaning as temporal transcendence: wanting to have an impact beyond our lifespan, beyond our own generation and age—the pursuit of which can help ease feelings of mortality that can otherwise cloud wonderful and fulfilling lives.

In this and other legacy-related efforts, there's also an element of wanting to "give back," perhaps hoping to balance the negative effects we've had on the world with positive ones.

Tycoons who oppress their workers to enrich themselves, then, might build libraries, and parents who terrorize their children might leave them hefty inheritances.

These efforts don't perfectly cancel out the (sometimes horrible) actions of those who invest in them, but it makes sense that even the non-spiritual (and thus, not afraid of post-death moral judgement by some kind of deity) among us might want to be remembered fondly, as a net-positive for the world rather than the opposite, even after a life seemingly devoid of such concerns.

Death has a way of refocusing our minds, and history is awash with examples of people whose priorities diametrically changed as they stepped into their latter, post-conquest years, swapping one set of success metrics for another at the existential last minute.

It's simpler and less effortful to focus on causing less damage and pain, to begin with, rather than scrambling to dilute a lifetime's-worth of carnage in our silver years. But our sense of purpose and importance changes as we change, and our last-ditch efforts to bring symmetry to our legacy are shaped by the paths we take to get there.

One way of thinking about leaving a positive legacy is to make the world better for those who come after us, whomever they might be.

We may complicate this (relatively simple) conception of legacy by asking ourselves whether we want to benefit all of humanity or just "our people"—those we consider to be like us, who come from our home country or town, or those with whom we share a faith or currency or collection of norms.

We might also attempt to categorize some people as deserving and others as less or undeserving of our beneficence, directing our charity or humanistic acts toward those who work, those who vote like we vote, and so on.

For things to get better for those who come after us, though, future humans (and the societies in which they live) will need to be unfamiliar; we can't expect positive change if they're just like us, their lives shaped by all the same ideas and variables as ours.

The categories and considerations we might use to carve up humanity may not apply to our descendants, then, and if we actually want the best for them, they'll need to surpass us, to be elevated beyond the concerns, biases, and limitations of the present.

There's a tendency to celebrate some of the horrible things we suffer, promoting them as lessons and opportunities rather than as the unnecessary punishments and sources of pain they actually are. This is a psychological defense mechanism that allows us to move forward and recall traumatic experiences as something positive, which can be useful, but inflicting those same burdens on our successors (usually in the name of tradition) is more akin to hazing than tough love: it's generational agony we thoughtlessly enforce on strangers because we endured the same.

Sometimes this will mean physically harming children as part of a cultural ritual, and sometimes it will mean cleaving to a system of governance, economics, or social organization because we find it difficult to imagine doing something else, even if better, less-torturous versions have become thinkable and workable since their original implementation.

It may be possible, then, to establish a positive legacy by simply getting out of the way and allowing things to change, even if these changes make us uncomfortable, conflicting with our current norms and sense of what's right and proper, and even if we worry about the future and the decisions the people who will live in that future may make (in contrast to the choices we would have made).

There's a thin line between doing things to contribute beyond ourselves, and doing things because of ego, and this applies to large-scale undertakings like building a skyscraper, but also humbler acts, like having kids.

Just like inventing a new technology or making a scientific breakthrough, by having children, we influence the future. Our children have uncapped potential, and the legacy we can establish through them is similarly unbounded.

It's possible to positively impact the world and future generations without having children, though, as people of all ages need friends, needs chosen family, need mentors, need aunts and uncles, blood-related and otherwise.

We can choose to positively shape other peoples' lives in countless ways, and we can do so without procreating because our every action ripples into the future, leading to consequences for individual humans and, in some cases, all of humanity.

Our capacity to spark such staggering volumes of change can be intimidating, but it's also empowering if we decide to wield it purposefully.

Our motivations for transcending our mortal eras vary, as do our justifications for this transcendence and our psychological framings of what it means to do so.

If we can temper our self-serving motivations and focus on those that empower rather than limit future generations, though, we can convert our lifelong, purpose-seeking energy into truly meaningful, broadly beneficent outcomes, whatever shape our efforts take.

Accumulation

One definition of minimalism is focusing on what's most vital so that we have more time, energy, and resources to spend on the important things.

What's important to each of us will vary, as will what feels like clutter. Our sense of priority will also change as we change: increases in age, experience, and knowledge all potentially rerouting us from one set of essentials to another.

We experience such segues over and over throughout our lives, and it's thus prudent we learn to manage our possessions even as our relationship with them (and the world beyond them) continues to evolve.

As we grow and do and learn and iterate, we accumulate things.

Not in a hoarding sort of way, but in a conventional, socially acceptable manner: we make purchases, we receive gifts and inherit things, and we're handed doodads (and e-doodads) by companies and strangers and the winds of random happenstance.

We consequently come to own stones and shells from beaches we've visited, smartphones that house a portfolio of apps we've downloaded and photos we've taken, and the dining room table we bought when we realized we might want to have people over for dinner someday.

That's alongside all the pens and pencils, the forks, the extra sauce packets from our favorite fast-food joint, the medicines in our cabinet, the books we read, the shoes we wear, and the art we have on our walls.

It's a lot of stuff! And our personal hoards seem to accrue of their own volition, each addition making perfect sense in isolation, but then becoming an atomic unit of the larger, sprawling mass as we move on to the next necessity of the moment, the next justifiable accretion, and at some point we realize we own more than we need and don't know how to deal with that fact.

This is a recurring process, and cleaning out the junk drawer once won't necessarily result in a lifetime of spartan tidiness or a sense of accumulatory control.

It is possible to avoid inflating our hoard beyond what's purposeful if we develop habits that help us check ourselves over time, though, and that then allows us to establish more sustainable and effective maintenance practices, however our circumstances or priorities might change in the future.

Fundamental to implementing such habits is understanding that it's more important to manage our inputs than our outflows, at least at first.

In this context that means focusing on how we accumulate things rather than trying to scale-down our existing pile of possessions, because it's impossible to bail out a sinking ship while continuing to pump water into the hold, adding more than we subtract.

Committing to de-cluttering and getting rid of things will only get us so far, then, and it's arguably more important that we develop a healthy approach to consumption before we start thinking about what needs to go and what should stay.

The basic concept of minimalism can help here, as focusing on what's most vital, what's more important than anything else in our lives, can do wonders for helping us spend on the right things ("right" according to our priorities), but it can also be helpful to adopt tactical heuristics like a "one in, one out" policy (getting rid of something every time we bring something new into our lives) as some consumption-related decisions will be spur-of-the-moment, and it's sometimes easier to catch ourselves when we've got concrete, if-then decision trees worked out for such moments ahead of time.

Another filter we might apply to potential acquisitions is asking about opportunity costs rather than just sticker prices.

A new smartphone might cost $1,000 (a fair bit of money), but what we're giving up—all the other things that money might buy us—can be even more perceptually hefty than the dollar value itself.

A thousand bucks could pay for a vacation, a month's rent (or other such expenses), new tires for the car, many bags of groceries, several new outfits, or even another gadget, like a laptop.

Buying that phone doesn't just mean losing that money, then, it means trading away all those other things we could get, instead, and reminding ourselves of this before making a purchase can put that purchase into a more complete context.

We might also adopt a policy of spending more on experiences and expendables, and less on goods that stick around and take up space.

That means opting to invest more in food with friends and the nice coffee beans we really like instead of more clothes or gizmos or other things that might seem appealing, but from which we wouldn't derive as much value.

This can reorient our priorities away from stuff that accumulates into piles and toward things that help us survive, thrive, and amass fond memories.

One more tactic is to remind ourselves of disappointing purchases we've made in the past that seemed like great gets when we were buying them, but which we then relegated to a shelf or dark corner of the closet where to this day they gather dust and serve no purpose.

Even with all the front-loaded care in the world, there's a good chance we'll still accrete drawerfuls of possessions because our needs change, we relocate and have to buy apartment-sized bundles of stuff all at once, or because we adopt a pet, have children, or move in with a partner who has their own things and their own wants, needs, and approaches to dealing with what they own and will someday own.

There's no perfect, always reliable way to establish stuff-related balance with a partner (or other person with whom we share space), but it's generally beneficial to establish and maintain open, understanding, and nonjudgemental lines of communication and to make our needs clear, do what we can to help meet their needs, and avoid proselytizing or demonizing (even if their clutterful habits clash with our pile-free preferences).

It's also worth noting that for some of us accumulation is a habit inherited from people who have lived through leaner, less-certain times and who thus consider holding onto things an existential imperative.

People who have survived economic depressions or other circumstances in which fundamentals were in short supply or out of reach may hang on to furniture and appliances and all manners of knickknacks because those who did so, when they were younger, were the ones that did well, and they want to offer their loved ones that same good fortune.

Many such people are realizing, though, that their kids don't want the things they've been accumulating on their behalf because they already have their own furniture and appliances (and too many knickknacks); the stuff that's waiting for them in basements and storage facilities will wait there until the caring and diligent archivists who tucked them away pass on, all that stuff becoming one more responsibility that their survivors will have to deal with when they're gone.

There are ways to get unused goods into the hands of people who actually need and will derive immense value from them, though.

Buy Nothing and similar groups (most of which are on Facebook and other social networks) help people who need things connect with neighbors who have things, enabling a localized, cyclical gift economy that gets un- or under-utilized goods off shelves and out of closets and into productive service, while also building new connections between folks who might not otherwise have any reason to interact or share with each other in this way.

These groups also help temper the production of unnecessary goods and reduce the waste associated with the making and purposeless purchasing of the same, which makes them one of the better ways to deal with our existing clutter after we've addressed our accumulation inflow.

But Maybes

As we mature, there's a tendency to accept more things that we may have previously raged against and fought.

This acceptance can be a healthy consequence of experience-derived wisdom, as slamming our heads against the same problems over and over won't always result in solutions, nor the removal of what vexes us.

It can also be exhausting to maintain an anger-fueled vigilance, dedicating ourselves to being upset about, for instance, a health issue we were born with and for which there isn't any treatment or cure, or the persistently abysmal state of national politics in our home country.

These are issues for which there might never be a true remedy (short of death or revolution), so coming to acknowledge their continuity can release some of the pressure that might otherwise build up, allowing us to decompress and achieve a more sustainable, equalized state of strain.

I would argue, however, that it can also be healthy to leave room for "but maybes" rather than completely dismissing an issue as unfixable, unrightable, and unreconcilable.

In this context, leaving room for "but maybes" means coming to accept things that are probably locked into place, but for which there theoretically could be some kind of solution at some unpredictable point in the future.

There's no treatment or cure for our condition today, but maybe something will change tomorrow, ten years from now, or in a handful of decades.

Our politics are stuck at an impasse, but maybe a new technology or cultural movement will enable a new model of governance, allow more voices to be heard, or nudge us toward a collaborative ideological climate.

I think it's important to maintain a sense of hope while also striking a psychological stance that acknowledges the facts on the ground today—those facts likely fixed in place for the foreseeable future.

Throughout history, though, we have changed or eliminated negative (to us) aspects of life, even when there was no reason to believe these elements would ever cease being permanent fixtures.

That can and will happen again, and it's possible that whatever variable we hope will change will, in fact, change, and possibly soon enough for us to enjoy the consequences of that evolution.

But it also might not.

Revolutionary transformation is seldom predictable, and it's best to operate as if the variable that plagues us will remain immutable.

If we act under that assumption and plan based on that likelihood, but can still leave room for the opposite—for hope—we'll be okay whatever happens, and even small, positive changes to that oh-so-despised variable will serve as pleasant surprises.

Grief

The older we get, the more likely we are to have experienced —or to be actively experiencing in a given moment—grief.

At its core, grief is an emotional response to loss; losing someone we care about, losing an object, losing a status quo, or feeling remorse as we're deprived of a non-tangible, non-entity, still-cherished (or taken for granted) circumstance.

One of the key elements of what's often casually referred to as a midlife crisis is the slow-motion psychological disaster of seeing our parents incrementally succumb to the vicissitudes of age. They physically degrade, are not as cognitively sharp, maybe they pull back from the world, become set in their ways and grow withdrawn and irritated —maybe even angry at a society that no longer makes as much sense to them because they've retreated from it and because they're navigating a mire of internal, senescence-linked debasements.

We may feel a deep-seated, difficult-to-pin-down remorse about this transition, about this change that inflicts pain on our loved ones, and everyone around them by association. And it may be a grief that's distinct from (but akin to) what we will someday experience when they die.

Seeing our friends or pets or significant others go through difficulties may also trigger this response: our own pain, our own trials, our own slogging path through the muck of life is one thing, but catching the reverberant agony of the same, secondhand from those we care about, is a distinct flavor of suffering.

This category of distress becomes more common the older we get because the people we know, our friends and family, and even our more distant associates and relations will tend to be older, on average, as we become older.

The more years we pile on, the more meaningful people (and other entities and norms) we accumulate, and the deeper those we maintain become. We've had more time and opportunity to build connections and establish valued habits and routines, and eventually all structures and systems degrade, decline, and degenerate. The load-bearing elements of our realities entropy from their first moment of existence, and that accumulation of dents, scratches, scars, and irreversible molecular disorder ultimately catches up with everything and everyone.

Grief, whatever the immediate source, can be contagious. It's unpleasant and sad and anxiety-inducing to see a loved one suffer, and we can experience vicarious grief just from knowing that someone we care about is near-drowning in their own sorrow.

We might also stumble into grief when going through periods of life-changing upset, whether the operational variables are extrinsic—war, famine, economic tumult, the emergence of new technologies that leave us jobless or forced to reeducate—or intrinsic, like the realization that we don't believe what we always thought we believed, or a change in priorities that leads to broken relationships, the reassessment of core tenets of who we assumed ourselves to be, or a relocation that requires we start over in an unfamiliar place.

Because of its many sources and faces, some of us become familiar with grief at an early age, while others are fortunate to establish a slow-drip familiarity with it over the course of our lives.

However we stumble or segue into it, though, grief is an unavoidable aspect of the human experience that becomes more common the more years we accrue, so it's prudent to be aware of its influence, to grow comfortable with its diversities of discomfort, and to understand how we optimally cope with it—incorporating grief into our lives and selves without surrendering to its depressive influence.

We respond to different varieties of grief in different ways, and our personal responses will vary over the course of our lives, as well.

There's evidence that people who are more prone to depression or anxiety may have a harder time wrestling with grief, as might people who have PTSD and associated disorders.

Most advice from experts in this space suggests we learn to acknowledge what has happened or is happening, that we allow ourselves to mourn (the loss of someone, a change in circumstances, etc), that we figure out us-shaped coping mechanisms that serve us both long- and short-term, and that we work toward establishing new norms that incorporate the relevant changes into our contextual perceptions and next-step plans.

Our coping mechanisms will be distinct because we are all different people, but what we reflexively think is best while grieving won't always be ideal: we might feel inclined to pull back from the world, when being around people will actually help us move forward faster; we may rebel against the idea of moving forward at all, when the best thing we can do for ourselves, for those around us, and for the memory of someone we lost (or a path or belief we're leaving behind) is to incorporate that broken thread into whatever design we weave, next.

Rather than hiding or burying painful realities, then, leaving ourselves prone to emotional landmines when future circumstances unearth unresolved emotions (our lives thenceforth punctuated by explosions or implosions sparked by triggering memories), it may be better to look our new situation square in the face, and mourn and remember and get angry and cry as much as we need to (ideally with support from our families and friends, from mental health professionals, and/or from people who have gone through similar things).

From there, we alchemize our pain into fuel. We use it as a motivating force to carry us into a new state of being that's different, but (if we approach the transition intentionally) better than what came before.

Work

Work means many things to us over the course of our lives.

It's the things we make, for money and otherwise.

It's something we do; it's how we spend our time, where we invest our energy and attention.

Work also, at least partially, defines us.

This isn't inherently the case, and the degree to which we seem to be little more than our jobs varies from place to place (and has varied over time, too).

But across many countries, cultures, and industries, today, one of the first things we ask and are asked about is "what do you do?"

This isn't how things have to be, but it is how things tend to be. And this will continue to be the case until we rethink our societal priorities, economic systems, or the rules we apply on an individual or communal level.

It's become a truism that the things we consider to be the least important of all our creations, and in which we take the least pride, will be the things for which we're best known, respected, and celebrated.

Thus, actors become known for their most mainstream and generic roles, writers are remembered for their earliest (and thus, least mature) books, artists attain notoriety for their least challenging periods, and so on.

This same concept applies to any work we might do, though rather than becoming known for cultural outputs, we might become known as "the accounting woman," or the guy who's a lifelong teacher; we're pigeonholed for work we've done that doesn't represent the full expanse of who we are, what we care about, and what we're capable of.

There's nothing wrong with being celebrated for things we don't particularly care about, but when that recognition prevents us from trying new things, it can be annoying, it can hinder our growth, and it can force us to decide between success in a space in which we're no longer interested, or less success (perhaps to the point of being unable to make a living) in the domains we actually care about.

I worked hard to avoid becoming the "travel guy" in my late-twenties, because while I enjoyed travel (and joyfully oriented my whole life around it), I also knew that I didn't want to be beholden to a single way of living my entire life. I didn't want to wake up one day in my forties and realize I could never slow down or hold still for even a minute, because my income, my reputation, my well-being and security were reliant on doing something that was interesting and valuable to others, but which had become dull and anchor-like, to me.

It took years to reorient my persona, my reputation, my body of work, and the expectations of my audience so that I could dabble more broadly, and there were economic, reputational, and other costs to doing so. But I see this as having been a worthwhile investment, as it allowed me to learn and do and become a lot more than would have otherwise been feasible within that earlier, comparably limited niche.

The model of employment that emerged in the mid-twentieth century motivated many people to get an education, take a job, and then stick with that job (or bare-minimum, the company that hired them) until retirement.

This model has disappeared, along with the loyalty companies extended to their employees, and the loyalty those employees often extended to their employers in return.

Post digital-revolution, the single-job, single-employer career track has given way to an array of practices, most of them oriented around temporality, change, and uncertainty.

What that typically means for employees is that our professional footing is tenuous at best, changing jobs regularly is a normal and sometimes desirable thing to have on our resumes (as it shows we have options), and that because of the semi-regular upending of entire industries, it may be prudent to maintain side-hustles and consider alternative career ladders.

You may be an accountant, today, but if your employer replaces you with software or you lose your interest in the job, it doesn't hurt to have other options.

We are capable of so many things, but because of how the work-world functions, many of us commit most of our time and effort to just one narrow, siloed set of skills and knowledge.

We might benefit, then, from thinking of ourselves as generalists who happen to be doing accounting work at the moment, rather than accountants, thus giving ourselves permission to explore broadly, invest our time, energy, and resources in things that don't currently earn us money, and to consider those outside, non-work efforts to be just as legitimate and self-defining as the labor we do to buy groceries and pay the rent, today.

This re-designation can also help us navigate the crisis many people experience when they lose their jobs or retire, because if we define ourselves in terms of our jobs and careers, alone, we're left with an undeveloped, maybe even hollow sense of self when those jobs or careers go away.

Another benefit of becoming a generalist is that it can help us develop a more accurate sense of self because we have more variables, interests, ideas, and knowledge to help us triangulate what we like, how we prefer to spend our time, and what we value.

Learning, experiencing, and trying more things, then, helps us develop a detailed map of all the things we could do and become, and that aids us in identifying (with heightened specificity) how we should actually spend our time for maximum impact, fulfillment, and happiness.

There's no single career path that will make everyone happy, and there's no right or wrong way to decide between the many things we could theoretically do, both to earn money and for our own development and enjoyment. But allowing ourselves to think expansively about both categories of effort grants us more options and helps us maintain a more flexible mindset, which puts us in a far more favorable position, whatever comes next.

Augmentations

I've reached an age at which people periodically ask if I've had work done.

This is at least partially because I wear sunscreen and moisturize (or so I tell myself), but it's also the consequence, I'm certain, of how common plastic surgery and other physical augmentations are when you reach an age at which some of the youthful benefits your body once provided for free begin to break down, diminishing or disappearing unless they're intentionally reinforced.

In some cases, this will mean treatments, drugs, or injections, and in others, it will mean the installation of shaped silicone to replicate (or outshine) non-silicone body parts.

We paint and plump and yes, moisturize ourselves to the best of our ability, and we do this because losing the visual appearance of youthfulness can suggest aging, but it can also hint at unhealthfulness, resulting in the loss of a specific type of status and glow that's maintained by preserving the aesthetic indicators of vitality and vigor for as long as possible.

Because of this depletion, many of us do healthful, silly but harmless, and sometimes legitimately dangerous things to maintain the veneer of youth, and it's impossible to discuss aging without addressing this facet of growing older, because the pressure to adhere to these visual standards is potent and pernicious.

Anything we might do to our own bodies, any adjustments we might make, any clothes we might wear, cosmetics we might apply, surgery we might elect to have, or drugs we might take to alter ourselves in some desirable way, are neutral decisions, not moral ones.

We have every right to get nose jobs and calf implants, to wear eyeliner and get hair plugs, for mainstream justifiable reasons or for no reason at all. Any accusations of vanity— that we should be ashamed for not aging in a way that other people feel is correct or appropriate—says more about those doing the accusing than it does about us.

It's notable that few people would criticize a 30-year-old man for growing and maintaining a beard because his partner thinks it looks good on him, but many feel comfortable criticizing an older woman who opts to color her hair, or an older man who gets a facelift.

The ease with which we decry the latter group of people who want to look a certain way, while not criticizing the former, reeks of agism, and the simplest way to make sure we're not succumbing to the urge to police other peoples' actions (in age-specific ways, or otherwise) is to remind ourselves it's really none of our business what other people do to their own bodies.

That said, even if we prefer to shave this and color that and tone, trim, and slim various aspects of our physical selves, we're ideally also comfortable with our own raw forms, and we make adjustments because we get some kind of satisfaction from doing so, not because we must in order to feel attractive or desired or loved or okay.

This can be easier said than done, of course, because of the many social and even economic pressures to adhere to certain aesthetic baselines and sensibilities.

This is something women have long dealt with (and in very substantial and life-altering ways), but it applies to everyone to some degree, even if we wouldn't consciously recognize the pressure to bathe, comb our hair, and not show up to work in stained and wrinkled t-shirts as socially enforced aesthetic coercion.

As we get older and our bodies change, we may face fresh pressures because our skin may wrinkle, our hair may gray, and our clothes may fit us differently; our aging bodies shifting stored fat to different locations, degrading our musculature, and overall disrupting our previous (far easier to maintain) status quos in all kinds of inconsiderate ways.

My response to these changes, so far at least, has been to acknowledge them as they arise, incorporate this information into my holistic sense of self and life—my perception of who am I, what I have to offer, what I like about myself, what I might improve upon, and so on—and then I decide whether and how to augment or upgrade things to account for stuff I don't like or that I find inconvenient or unpleasing.

This hasn't led to any major adjustments yet: I've got a simple skincare routine that I (finally) adopted in my early 30s, and I've adjusted my workout and eating habits to account for the things my body no longer does well, automatically, and to preempt changes I know are coming over the next few decades.

At this point I don't feel compelled to get plastic surgery or anything more substantial than trying out different moisturizers, but I also don't think it makes sense to rule anything out because I don't know who I'll be twenty years from now, and maybe that version of myself will be happy in every regard except for one stupid thing that I could easily remove (or add) with a quick trip to the doctor.

Living in the 21st century, we have access to an embarrassment of options when it comes to physical and mental augmentations.

Some of these upgrades (like hip replacements and laser eye surgery) address basic functionality issues, some (like smartphones) amplify our capabilities, while others are more cosmetic.

Access to all such tools is still incredibly uneven, but that availability grows each year, and that means an ever-increasing portion of humanity is being enhanced technologically.

Using these augmentations, we can buttress our weak spots and rebalance aspects of ourselves or our lives that have fallen out of equilibrium, and I would argue that the countless (and still growing number of) options we have for primping and prettifying ourselves are akin to those that allow us to more capably perambulate or seek knowledge and human connection, because they help us develop and maintain physical presences that we feel better align with our internal selves.

We should use such tools purposefully, though, rather than just rolling with whatever we're served, passively adhering to the norms of our societies, friend groups, industries, and cultural affiliations. These outside forces will happily tell us how we should be, how we should want to be, and how we thus must try to be, if we let them, and altering ourselves according to their preferences instead of our own makes it more likely we'll be socially acceptable, but a lot less likely we'll feel accurately represented by the shape we take.

Aging Out

As we get older, things that previously enlivened us may come to seem a bit ho-hum, folks we found interesting or entertaining might no longer scratch the same itch, and our tastes may change (in a culinary and in a cultural sense). We may replace our familiar habits with new ones, and our relationships can evolve into unfamiliar shapes.

It can also feel as if we're aging out of certain routines and expectations and goals.

While a younger version of ourselves may have aspired to the life of a famous performer or athlete, a version that's ten years older might be happy with owning our own home, enjoying a fulfilling relationship with a partner we love, or even just not experiencing persistent lower-back pain.

There are two things I try to keep in mind when I feel like I'm aging out of something.

The first is that while it can be startling and disconcerting to find that the same motivations, milestones, dynamics, habits, and entertainments don't do for us what they used to, these sorts of transitions are often markers of personal growth. Something in us has changed that prompted this shift, and that represents an opportunity but also a minor victory: we've grown.

And the second is that while it can sometimes seem constraining to no longer feel like we're the proper age to behave or crave as we once did, this transition isn't a strict, age-delineated mandate: we can revisit previously enjoyed pastimes, sensations, and goals and find fresh value in them, or recapture something of what was there before, even if we're perceiving them from a new angle.

Counterintuitively, this extraction from our prior state of being is more liberation than limitation, though we won't always see it that way until later, after we've had the opportunity to enjoy all the new things we've introduced into our lives to fill the gaps left by those earlier activities and preferences.

Many of us sleepwalk through portions of our lives, not because we're inattentive people, but because we all exist (to some degree) in the past, operating based on lessons and knowledge and heuristics (mental frameworks) derived from things we learned and did a long time ago.

Like a snake wandering around in skin that's become too tight, at some point we have to shed the version of ourselves that we were perfectly comfortable being until that moment. It's possible to wear a tight-fitting "self" for longer than might be desirable because there's seldom a clear impetus to get rid of it, and it's often easier to just keep slithering around in a familiar, if increasingly uncomfortable shape because metamorphosis can be exhausting, and it's disconcerting to wake up one day and find that we've changed, maybe fundamentally—but doesn't mean we shouldn't move on.

Aging out is really aging up: we feel like we're no longer part of a familiar paradigm because we're not—we've moved on to our next thing. That means we can look back fondly at what came before, but we can also perceive entirely new things that had long been invisible to us, and which, someday, we'll probably also shed and recall with affection.

Exposure

Just by existing, we grow and change.

That's true on a biological level, as external forces act upon our inherited epigenetic variables, stress our systems, and apply frictions to our physical selves—but it's also true cognitively and psychologically.

Every new experience, new person, new idea, new bit of knowledge, new understanding or sensation or discussion has the potential to flip one of our countless internal switches that can, in turn, spark small or fundamental changes to who we are, what we believe, and how we perceive.

These little pinpricks and epiphanies, these minor irritations and revelations, inform our personal evolution for better, worse, and (mostly) neutral.

We are who we are because of what we've learned and felt and done and had done to us. Recognizing this allows us to stack the deck in favor of more, and more beneficial personal iterations as we grow older.

It's possible, for instance, to optimize for more human connection, increasing the number, variety, and quality of our exposure surfaces so that we have relatively more opportunities to cross-pollinate with others.

In this context, cross-pollination means learning, teaching, and sharing knowledge, stories, and experiences with different people from different (perceived) groups.

It means recognizing that we have gobs to learn from those who are older than us, who have lived more life than we have (so far), but that there's also plenty we can learn from younger people, and people who are the same age we are, but who have lived dissimilar lives.

Expanding our relationships in both chronological directions, and befriending (and respecting) those who differ from us, can three-dimensionalize our perceptions while also helping us remain part of the story being written.

The alternative is stepping aside, witnessing life and the world from a distance, which means keeping all the things we might glean from others at arm's length, while also denying society all that we might contribute.

Extending ourselves in this way can seem like a tall order, because people who are older than us are boring and arrogant, thinking they know everything and that we know nothing, while those who are younger than us are cocky babies, obsessed with pointless trends and bizarre ambitions, right?

Such biases and assumptions are often more reflective of our own self-consciousness than reality.

Our elders lived through a different era, have been around long enough to see trends arise, play out, and fall back into obscurity, and have almost certainly solved puzzles we haven't even encountered yet.

People who are younger than us, though their spectrum of experience will be smaller, have likewise seen and done different things than we have, and thus know a lot we don't know, their perspectives shaped by that knowledge.

The same is true of folks with different backgrounds, faiths, educational resumes, fields of trade and levels of expertise, interests, personalities, relationships, familial dynamics, ethnicities, countries (and states or cities or streets) of origin, and every other attribute that's distinct from our own.

There's plenty to learn from someone who's almost exactly the same as us, because they will still perceive things differently than we do. Each distinction between us and those we encounter, though, increases the value we might glean from them and they from us.

Such exposure can be taxing because it's uncomfortable trying to understand information, ideas, and stories that challenge our sense of reality.

Our brains are prone to laziness and will do whatever they can to save energy, and one of their tricks is to build mental frameworks (often called "heuristics") of how things fit together and interoperate. These heuristics allow us to make decisions based on preexisting understandings of how the world works, serving as decision flowcharts that allow us to function without having to go into hardcore cognition mode every time we want to respond to a text or figure out what to eat for lunch.

When we encounter information that defies our mental models of the world, our brains push against that information, not liking the idea that they might have to change one of their beloved heuristics, and absolutely hating the idea that they may have been operating on faulty or incomplete information up till that point.

If we learn something we don't like about our political party of choice, for instance, it's often more psychologically palatable to ignore or justify away that information than to change not just the way we vote, but our opinions about political (and connected) issues, and maybe even our relationships that are predicated entirely or partly on that ideological affiliation.

This exposure, then, is often valuable in the same way exercising our muscles is valuable: it's for the better and strengthens us, long-term, but initially it breaks down what's there, and that can be uncomfortable and painful, which is why many people go to great lengths to avoid such experiences.

We can bypass this knee-jerk bias that favors the familiar and dismisses the unfamiliar, but it's not always easy, and it's possible to be influenced by it even as we attempt to correct for it; it's rooted deep.

I find it useful to nudge my brain toward curiosity whenever I feel myself harrumphing and becoming closed off toward (or offended by) something new (to me), as redefining ourselves as curious people can make it easier to engage with the unfamiliar in a neutral, less defensive manner.

Maintaining our connections to the world and to other humans is important for our health and capacity to grow, as without those connections we lack not just the psychological benefits of bonds and affiliations, but also the raw materials that allow us to change course when necessary or desired.

Not everything old is bad or good, nor is everything new inherently positive or negative. But some things are worth preserving, some things are worth adopting, and some things are worth blending and alchemizing into other things, to ensure they persist (even if not in their original shape).

We can't help determine what stays, goes, or changes if we don't understand and carve out spaces for ourselves within these new paradigms, though, and that means finding something to appreciate even in things that annoy or confound us, and putting in the effort to expose ourselves to growth-inducing forces throughout our lives.

Comparison

The grass, it's said, is always greener on the other side of the fence.

Part of why we want green grass in the first place, though, is that other people want it (or we believe they do).

Mimetic desire says we sometimes shortcut our decision-making process by looking at what other people do and then adjusting our behaviors accordingly. When other humans seem to want something, that tells our brains that the thing they want must be desirable, so we should probably want it, too.

If we take a moment to question that desire we can usually short-circuit this reflex, but left to their own devices our brains are lazy, doing whatever they can to save energy, and borrowing the (assumed) cognitive effort of other people's brains is one way to do that.

There's also a social component to this tendency, as we sometimes ape the people who belong to groups we'd like to belong to, or those we associate with ideas or movements or brands we'd also like to be associated with.

Thus, if a celebrity, community leader, or parent subscribes to certain ideologies, aims for certain goals, or wears certain labels (on their clothing or in their politics), we'll be more likely to subscribe, aim for, or wear the same.

These borrowed desires can spark new desires, or they can amplify existing wants.

They can also motivate comparison, as checking out what other people have got or are pursuing allows us to contrast our possessions and goals, looking for distinctions, and that can lead to even more angst when we realize this other person has things we don't, has done things we haven't, and is closer to their goals than we are to ours.

Comparing ourselves to others in this way is a losing game.

Doing so reinforces the internal sense that we're only good if we favorably measure up to others, which leaves us reliant on constant external validation.

Such comparisons will almost inevitably leave us feeling diminished, too, because we're contrasting our more complete, complicated, internal lives with the favorably filtered, share-worthy, well-edited external lives of other people.

More ideal is comparing our current selves with our past selves, focusing on areas of growth and progress. It also helps to maintain an awareness of areas in which we might improve—"improvement" gauged within the context of ourselves, not the context of all humans, because we have different variables acting upon our lives and capacities, so two people doing exactly the same things in the same way will still achieve different outcomes through no fault or virtue of their own.

Cultural expectations about who we should be, where we should be, and what we should have accomplished at different ages can also inflame and amplify comparative urges.

At this age I should have finished my education, at this other age I should have my own apartment, by the time I'm x-years-old I should own a home, by the time I've turned y I should be married with my first kid, and so on.

We often inherit these expectations from well-meaning people in our lives, from pop culture, and from our peers, and they rarely line up with our personal wants, needs, capacities, or resources.

Adopting a cookie-cutter portfolio of goals and an order in which we should implement them is a sure-fire way to stoke stress and strain, and can drain huge volumes of time, energy, and resources as we pursue things we don't actually care about, but which we feel compelled to accomplish at specific moments in our lives.

Many of our psychological issues, however old we are, stem from gaps between what we want and what we have.

Developing a better sense of which goals make sense for us (and when to pursue them) can narrow some of those gaps, while also helping us cope with their existence in a healthier and more sustainable way.

Health

Health is a staggeringly huge topic, so I'm going to break it up into more tackle-able segments.

Let's start with a big picture conception:

Health is a multi-faceted, inherently distributed and interconnected thing. It's not something anyone can sell you. There's no single source of health issues and no single solution that brings good health. A whole body, mind, and life focus is required if we want to approach health intentionally.

We have to decide to prioritize our health if we want to keep it: the older we get, the more difficult it becomes to maintain.

Fundamental to such prioritization is focusing on our core, and that's true in the literal sense of ensuring we have healthy torsos, but also in the sense that there are many structural variables that can negatively or positively influence our health, and assiduously working out and eating will not lead to the outcomes we desire if we don't attend to these central, interior elements in parallel.

One core concept worth understanding is that our bodies and minds need to be stressed, strained, and pushed in order to operate optimally.

This defies the intuition that avoiding stressors and frictions is desirable. Who, after all, wants to be inconvenienced or exhausted? Who wants to think strainfully and be pushed to their psychological limits?

In the modern, rich world especially, many of us will go far out of our way and pay colossal sums of money to avoid any kind of perceptually unnecessary labor or effort. Purveyors of goods and services are happy to assist us in this ambition, smoothing down even the most minute impedances so that we enjoy a truly seamless, smooth consumption experience.

But without gravity our bodies go haywire: our bones thin and our muscles atrophy, our cardiovascular systems—which are optimized to fight gravity's downward pull—send blood where it shouldn't go. Our sinuses are blocked, our backs, no longer supporting the expected weight, chronically ache, and our thinking becomes fuzzy.

Many people feel depressed when they no longer have work to do or responsibilities to fulfill, and unexercised brains become rigid and averse to change. Lacking challenges, exercise, and the excuse to flex and struggle, our minds may invent problems to solve and hardships to fixate on.

We require opportunities to exert our bodies and minds, then, but we also don't want to push too hard or too consistently, lest we damage our tissue or plant the seeds for chronic stress or anxiety.

Not too much, not too little: we thrive on just the right amount of strain.

Thus, working out can be great for us, but too much exercise can achieve the opposite, seriously harming our bodies instead.

A little gravity is perfect for humans, but too much would crush our spines.

At a high enough volume, even vital, life-sustaining water becomes toxic.

The general rule here, then, is that we aim for the optimal measure of things, rather than defaulting to impressive-seeming extremes or passive absences.

Our bodies and minds are meant to be used, but we should use them at levels appropriate for flourishing, not those that lead to floundering or failure.

Moderation is key, then, balance is ideal, and equilibrium is fundamental to sustained thriving.

Another core component of our health is sleep.

The older I get, the more I prioritize a good night's rest.

Though in my teens and twenties I could sometimes convince myself I was fine with just four or five hours of sleep each night, eventually I realized how much better I felt and functioned when I got a full eight hours. I've since habituated getting to sleep early so I can wake up early, which is a general, though not universal trend: we're more likely to be night owls when we're younger, but most people experience a change in their circadian rhythms as they age, tiring earlier than they used to and becoming more alert and wakeful earlier in the morning.

Some of us have a natural inclination to be solid sleepers, others go through periods of sleep-ease followed by years of struggling. Some of us will have trouble falling and staying asleep throughout our entire lives, and all we can do is figure out ways to temper that tendency.

Every body and mind is different, but the research we currently have available suggests it helps to avoid screens, eating, and stressful activities (including exercise) a few hours before our intended bedtimes. It can also be beneficial to dim the lights and turn down the thermostat leading up to that moment.

The goal is to mimic the wind-down process our ancestors would have experienced, the temperature drop and darkness (from the sun going down over the horizon) telling our bodies it's almost time to hit the hay. Avoiding things that might rile us up, triggering fight-or-flight reflexes or activating our digestion or muscle-healing mechanisms, can also help our bodies calmly slip into a more slumberful rhythm.

Many of us take stimulants of some kind (like caffeine), and ideally we ensure they're out of our systems by this time of night (relegating coffee consumption to the morning is advisable). There's some evidence, too, that reading fiction before bed can help us pull our minds out of the real world and dampen potential stress-triggers, though doing anything we find relaxing may serve the same purpose.

Maybe most important, though, is establishing a relatively consistent sleep cadence so our bodies aren't forced to accommodate unpredictable schedules each night. The more we template this process, the better we sleep, all else being equal.

Again, many people struggle with this their entire lives, and there are countless conditions (physical and psychological) that can make sleeping more difficult, even if we do everything else right.

But figuring out an individualized setup for sleep and refining it over time is one of the more valuable investments we can make, as getting enough sleep for our needs most nights pays incredible dividends, influencing every aspect of how we feel and function.

The nature and quality of our relationships can also have a significant impact on our core health.

Everyone needs and wants different things out of each of their relationships, whether they're with other people, non-people entities (like animals and plants), places, communities, or concepts, so we have to customize (and periodically re-customize) each one to ensure it's fulfilling and valuable for everyone involved.

Our most central relationship is with ourselves, though, and it's important we develop our self-confidence while also developing a healthy sense of self-awareness.

As I write this chapter, I'm sick. My body is aching, my brain's a little mushy, and it's like I have an internal dashboard that's flashing warnings about the systems in my body that aren't operating at their full capacity.

This sounds like a small thing, but having a decent sense of what it feels like to be ourselves, neutrally, allows us to assess, with decent accuracy, what's going right, what's going wrong, and what aspects of ourselves might need some attention if we want to function properly.

This knowledge is useful when we're sick as it can help us tweak our habits, movements, and behaviors to accommodate our new (hopefully temporary) hobbled forms. But it's also useful after a breakup when we're emotional wrecks, when we're struggling in difficult to define ways, or when we're integrating a new workout into our exercise routine and are keen to avoid injuring ourselves as we ease into our new rhythm.

Here's how I feel before and after my first cup of coffee in the morning; here's how I feel after an argument with my partner (versus when we're having a good time together); here's how I feel when I've had a fulfilling, productive day, compared to when I've lounged around being unproductive (or compared to when I've been productive in non-work-related ways).

This is also valuable, of course, as we get older and our bodies and brains change (in what we might perceive to be positive, negative, or neutral fashions), and as we're attempting to adjust to those changes: reinforcing ourselves where we can, and learning to accommodate and live with the rest.

Taking the time to learn what it feels like to be ourselves when things are boring and normal, when we have no pressing reason to pay attention to such things, can be beneficial, then, as doing so gives us a baseline for comparison when things are going completely sideways, or when we're feeling just a little off.

This self-awareness can also help us recognize and appreciate what we do well, where we could use a little help or additional effort, and it contributes to our psychological well-being by granting us power over our own condition and development, while also helping us form more healthful and strong relationships with others (because we better understand ourselves, what we need, and what we can contribute).

Our external relationships also play a role in our health (or lack thereof) by helping us feel needed, useful, and like we're part of something bigger than ourselves; a medium-scale sense of transcendence that allows us to function as part of a friend-group, a family, or a community.

Investing in strong friendships and familial relationships plays a huge role here, but it's also possible to bake these sorts of dynamics into our lives by joining clubs, taking part in civic life, and even establishing multi-generational living situations or a "chosen family" living arrangement, sharing a home with a group of friends.

Anything we can do to build and maintain ties with people we like, who help us grow, and who fulfill us rather than draining us, can be an excellent investment. And while there are only so many hours in the day, committing some of that time to these relationships (in a way that resonates with our needs) is almost always a worthwhile expenditure.

These external relationships also help us develop our self-knowledge, because we partially perceive ourselves through the lens of how other people see us, and because the connections we have with other people and things create a sort of outline that maps onto our sense of who we are in a social context. Through these interactions, we strengthen the core of our self-awareness, even as we reinforce the ties that bind us to the world beyond our bodies and minds—all of which can contribute positively to our psychological well-being.

Some of us will struggle with this because of how we're genetically or neurologically wired, because of how we grew up, because of things we've experienced, or for no obvious reason at all.

It's possible to reorient ourselves toward a steadier sense of well-being, but outcomes will vary, and what we're really aiming for here is a general sense of wellness: it won't be perfect, it won't be constant, it will be different for everyone, and it will require maintenance.

A commitment to such maintenance determines a lot about how we feel and live, though, and makes it easier to sustain other positive health-related habits.

Such commitments are easier to make when we start from a baseline of not feeling psychologically fragile and drained, though, and something that I've found helps me when I'm struggling and feeling anxious, let down, or pessimistic, is to become more informed about whatever it is I'm worrying over.

There's research, for instance, that shows the more people learn about the environment and other components of climate change, the less climate-anxiety they suffer.

This isn't because there's nothing to worry about, it's because more knowledge means a better understanding of the problems we face and our capacity to face them successfully, if we choose to do so. More knowledge helps us think with nuance rather than purely in black-and-white, and it's in those gray areas that change and possibility thrive; knowledge is empowering, and empowerment can help moderate our emotional states.

I find the same to be true with the news and history: there's plenty to worry about pretty much always, but the more I know, the more I can assuage my purposeless anxieties about all the horrible (and potentially horrible) global goings-on with an understanding of just how complex everything is, and how many potential solutions and silver linings there are, alongside all the storm clouds.

This can help with anxiety and stress, which can help us feel more empowered, and that can ease the sense of helplessness many of us might otherwise feel, related to one specific thing or to everything.

Our perception of mortality can also be healthful or unhealthful, as it informs many aspects of how we live and plan, what we invest in, and what we consider valuable or worthless.

I would love to live forever if doing so in good health became an attainable option. I think this is theoretically possible and may even happen at some point in the future, though I'm skeptical the necessary knowledge and treatments will come of age before I die.

That said, thinking about how we would approach a theoretical immortality treatment can be valuable, as it can help us concretize otherwise fuzzy philosophies we might harbor about life, death, and how we value and think about both.

Whether we rely on sci-fi concepts, conversations with friends, therapy, or otherwise, having an internal conversation about the nature of non-life can neutralize some of the disquiet we might otherwise feel about the concept of our (currently unavoidable and possibility more finite than we would prefer) mortality.

I don't think there's anything inherently wrong with wanting to enjoy the benefits of life, and even physical and cognitive youthfulness, for as long as possible. But I think it's healthy to find a way to appreciate whatever we get (in terms of both years and our capacities during those years) and to love ourselves for the duration—however (and for however long) we look, feel, and cognate.

Lacking such comfort, we're more prone to disorientation and depression as our bodies and minds change, our sense of self is disrupted, and our relationship with the world becomes more tenuous.

All that big picture stuff in mind, let's spend a little time on diet and exercise.

Most of us have a general sense of how this works already, but there's a lot of noise and misinformation out there, so it's worth revisiting the basics.

Most research suggests that we should eat a range of different things, avoid anything too highly processed, opt for foods with natural flavoring when we can (rather than foods with powerful synthetic flavors that can numb us to the natural ones in healthier foods), and that we stay hydrated.

Folks who get more fiber and who eat primarily fruits, vegetables, and complex carbohydrates seem to avoid a lot of issues suffered by those who eat a lot of processed fats, sugars, and (especially red) meat, and nutrients are absorbed differently depending on how we consume them, the peculiarities of our bodies, and other sneaky variables; so some of us will need to eat more iron than others, some will need more calcium, and so on.

The general consensus is that it's almost always better to get nutrition through food than through supplements, but sometimes that's not an option, and most of us will lose body mass as we age, our bone density diminishing and our muscles shrinking, so engaging in activities and workouts that help us build both (alongside the right volume of calcium and protein intake) is prudent.

It's also a good idea to work our whole collection of stabilizing muscles and ligaments, rather than just wailing on individual muscles or muscle-groups (like our biceps or abs). It's prudent to get at least 150 minutes of moderate aerobic activity each week (or about half that of vigorous aerobic activity over the same period) and to avoid overstraining. And it's advised we slowly and carefully incorporate our workout routines into our lives, rather than enthusiastically jumping in and injuring ourselves.

After suffering an injury (or pain that implies we could be on the verge of an injury) it's recommended that we allow ourselves to rest and heal, and that we get medical care if warranted, rather than pushing through the pain (as that could lead to a bigger and more serious injury).

And while a combination of cardiovascular exercise and lifting heavy things is an excellent ambition, routines consisting of body-weight resistance exercises that can be performed anywhere and with no equipment (other than our own bodies) are also effective.

We're all different, we all have distinct ceilings and floors in terms of what we can and should do, physically, and different people doing the same things will achieve different outcomes.

But developing and incorporating some kind of exercise routine into our lives and performing them habitually, maintaining an intentional diet, and focusing on sleep, mental health, and relationships, are some of the better things we can do to enjoy and extend healthful, option-rich lives.

Seasonality

It's tempting to perceive ourselves as monolithic and unchanging, but the only truly consistent thing about human beings is our tendency to change. This is true at both micro and macro scales, and a collection of relatively minor changes can aggregate, over time, into truly substantial evolutions.

These larger developments can delineate entirely new phases of our lives, demarcating (for instance) our high school years from our college years, our early working lives from our early days as parents.

We can define such periods based on a whim, or on the significance of specific moments and the intervals containing them. Elements of our lives will change at different speeds and cadences, too, our relationships metamorphosing before our careers or our sense of meaning iterating before our culinary preferences.

Perceiving our lives as a sequence of seasons can be useful, as it redefines the changes we experience as something akin to the whims of the weather, or the transition from trees filled with green foliage to paths paved with red and orange leaves.

The world will change, we will change, and many of these changes will be uncomfortable, disconcerting, painful, and weird. Many will also be creativity-inducing, awe-inspiring, and fulfilling.

Viewing these progressions as natural can help us mentally recategorize what's happening as just something that happens, or a collection of unpredictable somethings, many of which we'll enjoy, some of which not so much. In either case, though, neutral occurrences about which we needn't feel any particular way, and which we can experience and respond to however we choose.

The seasons we live through as we age also provide us with the opportunity to break free of previous expectations, assumptions, and limits, liberating us to explore and experiment broadly, and to experience and learn and embrace new things—all of which provides us with raw materials we can use to construct the next chapter of our lives.

Aging thus becomes a process of growing less certain, but more confident over time, as we continue to encounter things that challenge our previous assumptions and paradigms, but which also remind us we can incorporate what we learn from these encounters into ourselves, growing from such exposure, rather than being compressed or reduced by it.

This perspective also encourages us to engage with new things productively, openly, and enthusiastically, as we never know what will be valuable to future versions of ourselves (people who may be similar or radically distinct from our current manifestations).

In this way, we become less likely to push away from new ideas, norms, and technologies, and that helps us maintain a foothold in the world, even as we continue to refine our sense of who we are in relation to everyone and everything else.

We are all lifelong projects, and one of our perennial tasks is noting the adversities with which we struggle so we can develop coping mechanisms, support systems, and solutions that'll later aid us with these otherwise persistent plagues.

If we struggle with financial issues, we figure out how to address and maintain that aspect of our lives. If we have health problems, have depression, or are not great with relationships, we note these things, pinpoint the flaws, vulnerabilities, misinterpretations, misunderstandings, or knowledge-gaps, and then with time—perhaps a long time, perhaps no time at all—we fill in those gaps, reinforce those weak-spots, and over the course of however many seasons it takes, rebalance how we live until we no longer suffer from these things (or at least not as much).

The goal is to arrive at a point in which we would not give up a year of the lives we've lived for anything, because we've learned and done and grown so much that we wouldn't want to lose any of our hard-earned maturation.

Being a Good Adult

One of the defining features of growing older is that (eventually) we become adults.

Our internal perceptions of this transition may deviate from that of society, and this evolution rarely arrives all at once; it's a process.

At age 15 we seem like adults to toddlers, in our 30s we probably seem like adults to teenagers, and by the time we reach middle-age there's a good chance we seem like adults to just about everyone (except those in their 70s who may still consider us to be scrappy, not fully baked versions of those they perceive to be adults).

However and whenever it happens, and despite the fits-and-starts nature of this transformation, it's worth considering what being an adult means, to us, so we can be good ones, rather than lackluster or failed versions of the same.

I don't plan to have children, but some of my siblings already have them, so my perception of what it means to "adult," using the term of as verb, is being a significant figure and positive influence in the lives of my nieces and nephews, and the lives of kids I'm not related to (my societal nieces and nephews) as well.

This is a variation of the "campsite rule," the idea that we should leave people we encounter throughout our lives better than we found them. To me, though, the impetus to live up to this rule with younger people is even more pressing than with other adults because I have more power and influence and knowledge and experience than those who are not as old as me, and that shifts the weight of many responsibilities to my shoulders when I'm engaging with them.

The goal, then, is to imbue my interactions and relationships with young people with positive, valuable "uncle energy," rather than being a deleterious influence.

To me, this means helping to provide stability and a sense of safety, inspiring growth, stoking happiness and joy, and helping a globe full of nieces and nephews realize their goals: not just the ones I believe are essential, but those they think are important, too.

This is an incomplete philosophy, as I'm new to the phase of adulthood into which I've recently wandered, one in which most people I encounter consider me to be an adult.

I'm also new to uncledom, and while I suspect that performing this role intentionally will be similar to being a good friend, a good partner, and a good member of a community, I also know there's plenty I haven't experienced yet and much I cannot fathom from my current perspective.

So I'm filling in the gaps with what I see working for other people (and what the amazing adult influences in my life have themselves done), but this is a work in progress for me, as it will be for most of us as we step into roles for which we're destined, and which we therefore might as well do as properly (and beneficently) as we can manage.

Healthspan and Lifespan

It's normal to fear death.

Even those of us who believe in some kind of afterlife, whether as a spectral extension of our conscious existence or as some kind of "energy returning to the source" setup, are justified in not wanting to die because death represents absolute, permanent change. It may mark the end of everything we've ever experienced or can experience; it's the ultimate ceiling on our capacity to do or feel or think anything as our current, physical manifestations.

That's a terrifying thought, if you sit with it. And most of us do sit with it, eventually.

Society, if not psychology, also motivates most of us to establish a sustainable resting state when it comes to thoughts about death.

If we were cognizant of our own eventual, unavoidable death all day, every day, we wouldn't get much done, wouldn't be competitive in terms of procreation, and wouldn't accomplish much doing or feeling or being—much living.

While death is something we know we will someday experience, then, most of us can generally relegate it to the musty attics and dark, dank basements of our minds the majority of the time.

That said, some people keep the fear of death closer at hand and wear it like a totem, allowing it to shape the life paths they take, the joy they're able (or unable) to experience, and the relationships they build or decline to invest in (because what's the point?).

Others bury the concept of death deep, either embellishing it with so much flowery narrative that its psychological impact is diluted, or simply refusing to engage with the thought of not being, of no longer existing; in both cases stumbling a bit when the reality of death becomes unavoidable in all its (sometimes horrifying) profundity and finality.

The average lifespan for a human being living in a wealthy country has jumped from around 49 years at the beginning of the 20th century to more like 77 years at the beginning of the 21st.

This figure varies substantially depending on where we live, what sorts of healthcare services (and insurance schemes) are available, our gender, our professions and hobbies, and our diets and exercise routines. This is a general average, not what any individual human being should expect for themselves.

But one thing worth taking away from this statistic is that our current sense of longevity, folks living into their 80s, 90s, and 100s, is a very recent thing; the normalization of living into our 70s is a 20th century innovation. So before WWI, before electrification, before things like antibiotics and trains, although some people lived a long time, the expected span of a human life was far shorter than it is today.

That's remarkable and cool and worth celebrating, but something that's not obvious from those numbers is the fact that, in recent decades in particular, our healthspan—the number of years in which we're healthy enough to live how we'd like to live, rather than being debilitated by the frictions and rust of age-related ailments—has also been increasing.

So while the scope of our average lifespan has essentially stalled-out since the turn of the century, leaving us with an average of seventy-something years in which to do everything we'll ever do, more of those years have become usable and enjoyable, rather than serving, in some cases, as symbolic gestures at life: years in which we're so enfeebled that we're incapable of taking care of ourselves, and in which we might suffer so many issues that we would prefer not to be alive.

The current gap between average lifespan and average healthspan (for people living in wealthy countries, as of the early 2020s) is around 10 years, that number varying based on the individual, but also how we define and measure the concept of "healthspan," a term that is still only a few decades old.

That gap has increased a bit in recent years because of issues like pandemics, the global spread of unhealthy diets, and a statistically relevant surge in various types of substance abuse. But as with lifespan, the general trajectory here has been an increase in healthspan, which in practice means we enjoy more years that are livable, not just survivable, on average.

There's a lot of money and brilliance being aimed at both spans right now, as recent discoveries have pointed us toward potential biological leverage-points that could allow us to boost one or both figures, diminishing (for instance) the commonality and impact of predominantly elder-experienced conditions like Alzheimer's. There are innovations that may help augment our bodily repair systems, refresh our cells, and tweak our systems so that they're similar (in terms of maintenance) to those of our teenaged and twenty-something selves.

The degree to which these explorations will bear fruit is up in the air, but I would argue it's remarkable and borderline miraculous that we've already made it this far.

Age is a burden in many ways, but how wonderful that we live in an era in which we (and an ever-growing percentage of the human species) can grow old, and that we can use and enjoy most of the time we have!

I would suggest, though, that while it's amazing that we live in an age in which such developments are arriving so rapidly, and that we should absolutely enjoy the benefits they provide (if we care to), it's still prudent to develop and maintain a healthy sense of our own mortality, rather than hoping or assuming these or subsequent innovations will allow us to kick the mortality can down the road indefinitely so that we never have to consider the reality of our own, eventual demise.

Whether we die at 49 or 77 or 300, that's still an expiration date.

Whether we enjoy 40% or 80% or 100% utility of those years, we will still die.

There's a chance someday we'll bypass the concept of mortality entirely, only dying if and when we decide to do so. I would love to see that happen, as I want to learn and do and enjoy my life as long as possible.

But for the foreseeable future, the inevitability of death remains one of the few things we all have in common, and which we must thus work into our sense of what life is: a period of existence punctuated by an ending that may arrive at any moment, and which may come sooner than we would prefer.

Reaching the point where we are comfortable with this, have embraced this, and have interwoven this truth into our holistic understanding of life, the world, and reality—even if we're not thrilled about it—is arguably one of the more fundamental and important journeys we must undertake as conscious, finite beings.

Some of us arrive at that state of psychological equipoise early in life, some of us never get there. But moving in that direction is worthwhile, if only to ensure our sense of beginnings and endings (and thus, our conception of the path we walk) is concrete and stable enough that we can confidently build whatever we want atop it.

Self-Perception

I was always an enthusiastic, precocious child.

That's how the adults in my life treated me, at least, and that's how I came to see myself: how I self-defined all the way up to young adulthood.

Our internal sense of self is counterintuitively reliant on the perception of others. We look out into the world, our environment, and our social spaces to see how we're treated, how we're categorized, how we're elevated or diminished, what we're celebrated for and what we're told we can't do, or at least not do well, and we use this data as evidence when forming our own self-opinions.

Being good at school and being categorized (and celebrated) as a kid who was good at school helped define my childhood, and some of my resulting character traits grew around a scaffolding of that conception—"I'm good at school. This is who I am."

Somewhere along the way, I woke up to find that I was too old to be precocious, that school was no longer even visible in the rearview mirror, and that the world had sorted me into new categories with different labels and expectations and assumptions. It took a while to parse all this novel data, to flip through that fresh harvest of mirrored information, and to use it to figure out who I was in this unfamiliar, time-iterated context.

We are all thus shaped, though some of us are more sturdy and stalwart in our opposition to those external, sculpting influences than I was, persistently insisting we're something other than what everyone and everything around us say we are (though that ardently defended sense of who we are is usually just shaped by a different, less-obvious collection of outside forces).

As we age, we change shape in the physical and mental sense, but also in terms of how we're perceived and how we perceive ourselves.

Weaving a cocoon around our lives and reorienting our many assumptions and identifications before arising anew, butterfly-like, can be a struggle: a struggle we hope will calibrate our lives with the selves we've become since our last transformation (and with the selves we're growing into).

Sometimes our reorientations will be off.

Sometimes the growing pains will be excruciating.

Sometimes the recalibration will barely be noticeable, akin to jostling all the furniture in the living room a few inches from their prior placement, resulting in no obvious changes but endless annoying (and painful) bruised shins and scraped ankles.

Fortunately, many such adjustments are barely noticeable because they happen iteratively over time: our evolutions spread so thin that we and those around us would be hard-pressed to pinpoint what changes have occurred and when.

Some progressions arrive all at once, though. This is especially true when we haven't taken stock for a while, our transformations piling up beyond our notice. When they ultimately arrive, it's like a thousand letters being hauled onto our porch by the mail carrier on the same day—each missive weighing nothing at all, individually, but in aggregate? Even just sorting through it all represents a significant and weighty undertaking.

As I write this, I'm reviewing a small accumulation of such letters.

I allow myself the time and psychological space to keep tabs on these sorts of things, but at some ages and some life moments even a tendency toward the assiduous skimming and filing of these inputs isn't enough, and a more focused period of reflection is necessary to fully parse the situation and put all these processed pings into proper context.

The most vital aspect of this routine is understanding that it happens in the first place, and the next most vital is knowing something about the mechanism through which it occurs.

Both external and internal factors have shaped who we are and will shape who we become.

These factors (intrinsic and extrinsic) also change over time, which makes keeping track of them (much less how they affect us) a significant endeavor.

We can struggle against these adjustments, clinging for dear life to who we have been at the expense of whomever we might become next. We can also lean into them, maybe getting them wrong, at least at first, and then feel rudderless like we don't quite fit in our own skin, in the lives we're living, or in the wider world.

With attention, effort, and time, though, we realize who we've become and that grants us some control over our freshly donned attributes and our relationship with the world, which can help us—if we're intentional about it and if we allow ourselves to accept and embrace our capacity for further change—lay the groundwork for who we'll become next.

Subtraction

Many of us have a predisposition toward additive solutions to problems, even when subtractive solutions would be more effective.

There are numerous potential reasons for this heuristic, including a seeming cognitive bias toward addition over subtraction, even though we can recognize the value of removing something to solve a problem when prompted with that potentiality.

As a default, though—and research suggests this is especially true when we're stressed or otherwise cognitively burdened—solutions that rely on adding something rather than subtracting are more obvious to us and are thus the solutions we favor.

This means when faced with overwhelm at work, rather than attempting to streamline our portfolio of responsibilities, we'll go on the hunt for new calendar apps or organizational software to help us rebalance the load.

When things don't coordinate to our satisfaction when we're rearranging our living rooms, we'll look for more elements to add rather than asking ourselves what we might remove to achieve our desired aesthetic and functionality.

There are obvious reasons for maintaining the structure of the current status quo when making such decisions. When we've already purchased a bunch of furniture and decor for our living rooms, opting to subtract a loveseat or framed photograph might represent a financial loss, triggering what's sometimes called the "sunk cost fallacy," which is another common psychological predisposition that nudges us toward avoiding the perception of loss at all costs, even when doing so leads to undesirable outcomes (and more loss).

This is unfortunate, as too much stuff—too many options, too many possessions, too many responsibilities or calories or focuses—is at the root of many problems we face, and well-intentioned additions meant to help ease the load (or manage the responsibilities, organize the stuff, etc) don't change the nature of what's happening, and may even compound what's already there.

Recognizing when subtraction is more powerful than addition can be beneficial if we then allow ourselves to act upon that understanding.

Realizing that a friend is draining rather than fueling us, for instance, can nudge us toward spending less time with that friend, freeing up hours and energy we can then invest in more healthful and balanced relationships.

Similarly, recognizing that a beloved project isn't achieving the outcomes we hoped for (financially, spiritually, or socially) can lead to a redelegation of time and effort, but only if we allow ourselves to acknowledge this is the case and then act accordingly.

In this context, subtraction is as much about adding valuable things to our lives as it is about extracting less-valuable (or valueless) things.

Removing a habit that's not doing what we had hoped it would do frees up time and energy for another habit (or unscheduled free-time), and slimming down our work-loads or social calendars liberates all that cognitive and physical energy for other, more productive things ("productive" according to our personal definitions for the term, based on our current wants and needs).

Like monetary investments we might make, the concept of compounding interest applies to the way we spend our time: the right habits, the right stuff, the right relationships will over time bear fruit far beyond their obvious, day-to-day benefits, and the same is true in reverse for the wrong ones.

What's "right" and "wrong" when it comes to these sorts of expenditures will change as we change and as the world changes, so it's important to check in with ourselves regularly, lest we miss an opportunity to extract or sub-out something that's weighing us down and keeping us from enjoying all that we might enjoy.

But fundamental to this concept is understanding that subtraction is a viable option when attempting to rebalance and optimize just about anything, and that most of us will ignore subtraction-oriented options because of baseline human biases.

We can defy these (and other) predispositions, but doing so requires conscious effort and an understanding of why we might want to in the first place.

Priorities and Responsibilities

One of the biggest benefits of aging can also be one of the biggest bummers: the slow accumulation of responsibilities.

Having more responsibilities can be great, as responsibilities tend to be accompanied by rewards. A job earns us money, having a pet or kids nets us love and satisfaction, and working with a community organization helps us feel more connected to our neighbors and neighborhoods.

But responsibilities also force us to be responsible for things, and these claims on our time and attention can sometimes be at odds with our other priorities.

We may want to prioritize our health, but work demands we commute, sit in front of a computer all day, and eat whatever we can conveniently grab between meetings.

We may want to focus on developing our friendships as we grow older, but taking care of our kids can claim our physical and mental capacity, leaving us exhausted when we manage to scrounge small spans of downtime.

Sometimes our priorities and responsibilities will align, as is often the case with caring for our offspring and progressing in our careers (if we're fortunate enough to be doing work we care about and to feel good about the rewards we're earning for performing our duties, at least).

Many times, though, our desires and obligations will be in opposition to each other, and our lives will become increasingly zero-sum as we continue to add more priorities into the mix.

This gets better in our latter years (I hear), as we stair-step our way into retirement age and as many of our work- and child-related responsibilities become less pressing. We're finally able to turn our attention toward the stuff we want to do, which may include family and work-like efforts, but possibly not, and possibly not as much or of the same type as before.

For most of our lives, though, this tension can be the source of psychological dissonance, contributing to periodic crises and a sense of wasting our time, being on the wrong path, or not living up to our potential.

It's possible to bring these elements into better alignment earlier, but doing so requires a lot of self-discovery and self-awareness. We also have to be willing to uproot elements of our lives that aren't helping us become more holistically fulfilled, and which aren't contributing to the regular refurbishment of facets of our lives that no long align in this way: hobbies that are draining rather than empowering and fulfilling, for instance, or work that no longer inspires us or pays the bills.

Pursuing such alignment isn't always straightforward, and it isn't always easy. Even determining which aspects of our lives are serving us (and which no longer are) can be a multi-stage journey: one that's complicated by concerns about whether our brains are trying to trick us into being lazy, whether the metrics we're using to measure our outcomes are the right ones for who we are today and who we're becoming, and whether the job we're doing, party we're hosting, or sport we're playing on weekends truly is no longer the right fit for us and what we hope and need to accomplish.

Relationships

Relationships are fundamental to human flourishing, and though we all vary in terms of what sorts, how many, and how potent and tight these relationships should optimally be, their centrality to our thriving (or floundering) is a rare constant, whatever our age.

A quick summary of my stance on relationships goes something like this:

I believe relationships can and should take whatever shape makes the most sense for the people involved, that we should ensure everyone is getting what they need and want from the partnership, and that we should maintain them through clear, reliable communication, and with enough flexibility that the bond can change as the people involved change.

I think it usually makes sense to build atop a baseline of friendship, to aim to leave people better than we found them (whatever the nature of our dynamic with them), to weave romantic gestures and psychological boosts into everyday life, and to discuss what happens if the relationship ends someday, ahead of time, in order to reduce the likelihood of catastrophic failure, and to increase the chances of salvaging the friendship.

Many of these loose policies apply to all sorts of relationships, from best friends to workplace acquaintances to life partners to those with whom we might have periodic, casual hookups.

The general idea, though, is to value people for who they are, to avoid pressuring anyone to be something they're not, to ensure there are strong communication channels (so needs and problems can be transmitted and addressed), and to do what we can to maintain malleability and an openness to change.

It's important to get comfortable with the concept of change, even in the most (seemingly) stable and static associations. Such shifts will happen whether we want them to or not, and attempting to lock a specific relational shape into place, or pretending it's a different shape than it actually is (through stubbornness or ignorance), can crack and eventually shatter a valued bond.

Personal flexibility helps alleviate this potential fragility, as does building relationships that inherently bend instead of breaking.

We ideally strike this posture internally, too, not just in our connections with others.

We will change, our needs will change, our goals and beliefs and priorities will change. Our habits will develop, and our bodies will, too.

Maybe we'll want more or less sex than we did when we were younger. Maybe we'll be more or less inclined to travel or socialize or take hikes or have quiet nights inside with our partners.

The more assiduously we track such changes and, vitally, communicate them to those we care about (even if we might feel weird about it, or worry what they'll say), the more likely we are to successfully work with them to tweak the relevant relational dynamics so they accommodate our iterating needs (if such accommodation is possible).

I think it's worth mentioning, too, that we'll have an abundance of relationships with non-human things, ideas, and places over the course of our lives, and many of these policies apply to those dynamics, as well.

Our pets will change and our relationships with them will change, and it's prudent to be aware of this possibility, notice when it happens, and adjust our behaviors accordingly.

Our relationships with places we've been and lived, ideas we've held dear and which inform the way we do things, and even communities and organizations and other social aggregations, will likewise change over time.

The better our perception of these changes and the more willing we are to accept the possibility of minor or major recalibrations in our associations with whomever or whatever, the more likely we are to find new footing with the minimum of confusion, discord, and heartbreak (for anyone).

The most valuable relationship we'll ever have, though, is our relationship with ourselves. And the nature of that relationship ultimately determines the success of all the others, because lacking a sturdy foundation, lacking a sense of where we're at and what we care about and where we're headed, it's impossible to know (and communicate) what we need, and to have a sense of how to healthily and sustainably give others what they need from us, today and in the future.

Bodies

Our bodies change over time; sometimes radically and suddenly, sometimes so slowly that even with the benefit of experience and hindsight, it can be difficult to pinpoint precisely what's different (even though we may feel confident something is).

In our early years, these changes are primarily growth-related, our torsos expanding upward and outward, our brains rearranging and eventually settling into their final form (structurally, at least), our physiques accumulating altitude and girth, our bones and musculature achieving adult-scale heft and density, our tendons and fascia creeping, ivy-like, across our inter-organ expanses, our adult teeth calcifying, and our sex organs blooming and maturing.

Every body is distinct, but we all experience some combination of these iterations, even if at varying intensities and sometimes in a different order.

Despite those disparities, the result of this "growing up" process is that our biologies are prepared (or as prepared as they're going to be) for propagation: our adult human forms optimized to protect and perpetuate our genes.

After all that growth and some time spent navigating our designated proliferation era, though, we step into a somewhat more precarious state of biological affairs.

There are many theories as to why we develop the way we do after our prime baby-making age, and one explanation is that we evolved to focus on successful reproduction, and because of this biological prioritization we burn ourselves out in that pursuit, leaving little fuel in the tank for later.

The years after we birth and raise our kids into functional human beings aren't as important to our bodies, then, because we've done what we're meant to do: we've achieved the biotic meaning of life. This marks the practical expiration date for a lot of our bodily equipment.

Our physical finitude wasn't really notable until recently, as most of our ancestors lived in periods in which a minor scrape could become infected and kill them, and in which dying from things like childbirth, exposure, and saber-toothed tigers was common.

Humans died young (on average and by modern standards) until just the past few generations, and before that, the wise old sage of the village may have been in her mid-30s, and the man who survived into his 40s might become a Methuselah-like legend.

So according to this (heavily simplified) framing of things, living beyond an explosive, procreation- and competition-focused couple of decades was unusual for most of human history, and it consequently hasn't been fully worked out in the evolutionary sense.

At some point in our primordial ancestors' history, though, behavioral evolution took the wheel because humans who survived for a while after having and rearing children would stick around with their family groups (and communities) and help take care of things: guarding the food, babysitting other peoples' children—basically serving as bonus parents, defenders, and repositories of skills and knowledge.

This would likely have been a huge advantage for groups that benefitted from the efforts and wisdom of such oldsters, so biology may have started re-optimizing for traits that kept people going a little longer, then a little longer still, and on and on until humans living into (what we now call) middle-age was no longer rare, and multiple generations started coexisting with each other.

The practical outcome of this, if this is indeed what happened, is that beginning sometime around our 30s, our bodies recalibrate for different things: fat aggregating in new and exciting locations, our muscles rearranging to favor a fresh array efforts, and our sex organs (and entangled systems) going completely haywire.

All of which can make our bodies, our physical manifestations, feel unfamiliar. Things that always worked one way, looked one way, felt one way, might suddenly work and look and feel another way, and that can be jarring and disconcerting.

Whether or not that aforementioned theory of how old people became a thing (despite nature historically having favored the opposite) explains how we came to be how we are, it helps to understand that part of why we go through these phases of biological life—our bodies becoming mutated versions of themselves without apparent cause—is that something inside us is always rearranging the furniture for our next, life-cycle aligned purposes.

There are chronological moments in which it makes sense to be overtly fit and youthfully appealing and capable of casually bouncing back from breaks and sprains and tears, and there are other, later moments in which it makes more sense to spend our finite bodily resources on contrasting ambitions and priorities, like unflashy maintenance tasks that make us more capable at some things, less primed for others, and which change us both physiologically and cognitively.

Just as a propensity toward acne (for some of us, anyway) in our youth can be an unwelcome manifestation of the chemicals flooding through our bodies, priming us for adulthood, our tendencies to ache a bit more, to accumulate fat and lose muscle mass, and to grow sluggish when responding to new information can be perceptual downsides of reorienting toward deeper sorts of thinking and a more fine-tuned control over our focus and priorities.

Age reallocates resources so that we're ready for a biological marathon, rather than a sprint.

It's not always easy going through these transitions, even if we understand their purpose. It's one thing to know, in theory, why our bodies are changing, and another entirely to live through such change, with all the anxieties, pains, and dings to our self-confidence that can arise from such tumultuous maturation.

Many of us respond to these transformations by augmenting ourselves in various ways, shoring up our capacities when they show signs of flagging.

There's nothing at all wrong with getting treatments or refining our skin-care routines or leaning more heavily on tools and services that allow us to fully enjoy the extra time that social progress, modern medicine, and natural selection have bought us; anything that helps us feel good, capable, and at home in our own bodies is worthy of consideration.

Something worth considering, though, is that a reliance on external variables (like a particular product or service) can tie our psychological (and potentially, physical) well-being to that lotion or injection or software, so it's worth asking ourselves how things like diet and exercise and mental health habits (meditation, journaling, other sorts of non-productized self-care) might serve as a balance-imbuing foundation, ensuring we feel good and comfortable as a baseline, whatever our age, while still allowing us to integrate external upgrades if we so choose.

Composition

We are biomes. Each of us is an ecosystem of microscopic critters and cells comprising a confounding array of ingredients, and accumulating even more (and even more varied) jumbles of tiny creatures and other bio-pieces over the course of our lives.

The process of aging, viewed through this lens, is a process of adding and subtracting. It's the building of new components, alchemizing elements into other elements, and continuously expanding the number of relationships, connections, and interactions between all those constituents.

We are also composed of the things we know, our understandings and values and beliefs and biases, the traditions, norms, and assumptions we inherited from our families, friends, and institutions of learning, and the media we consume, information we soak up, and random things we experience over the course of our lives.

Our relationships shape us and how others see us, treat us, value us, and interact with us. Our responsibilities and the things we do to measure up to those responsibilities, the work we perform, the routines we maintain, the things we want, and the stuff we make shape the ecosystems of which we're a part, but also shape us.

We are amalgamations of many things, but we also amalgamate. We can perceive disconnected pieces and curate, tweak, and rearrange them, creating harmonies where previously there was only disorder, discord, and chaos.

This isn't a casual effort, and it's not a part-time gig. This is the work of a lifetime, and it's broad in scope and potential meaning.

We manipulate our biomes through what we eat, where we live, the work and exercise we do, and the people and animals and flora we come into contact with.

We adjust our intersections and exchanges with other humans and with society by coming to know ourselves, calibrating how we spend our time, energy, and resources, and adjusting our circumstances and environments to better align with our priorities, even as we adjust ourselves (our priors and habits and dynamics) for the same.

We create and are the creations of uncountable variables.

We are composers and the composed.

We are the conductors of the orchestra, and we are the music that's played.

Recognizing our nature and accepting the responsibility and power we wield is one of the many tasks we face as we learn and grow, as we catch glimpses of the previously unseen players and instruments, and as we attempt to capture the tune we've long been humming in all its (potential) symphonic splendor.

Regret

I recently paged through a handful of my older books, some of which I wrote more than a decade ago, recording fresh audiobook versions while making tweaks and copyedits along the way.

Some of what I wrote holds up remarkably well, but I have a lot of quibbles with how I presented my ideas and arguments, and even more about what I focused on and wrote about.

These are books I was proud of when I originally wrote and published them, but with each new volume, each year that passes—each time-delineated chunk of thinking and writing and sharing—I find them to be less a source of pride and more a source of something close to embarrassment. They no longer accurately represent me, even if they're still (thankfully) valuable to some people who read them and who are encountering those ideas and stories for the first time.

I try to go easy on myself when I look back at my past work and experiences because usually they were the best I could do at the time, and if even they weren't, they still served as lessons that taught me how I might do better in the future.

I regularly remind myself that being unhappy with my earlier efforts, both of the publishing and overall living variety, shows growth. Such regret is the consequence of having moved forward, and the gap between my earlier and current selves is the source of my discomfort and disquiet.

Some regret goes deeper than this, of course.

There's the question of what might have happened had we bought that stock we were eyeballing right before it doubled in value, or if we had rejected the marriage proposal that, once accepted, informed the subsequent nature of our lives.

I have those sorts of thoughts sometimes, and though most of them are small and piddly—what if I had said one thing instead of another during that awkward conversation? What if I hadn't made that purchase that turned out to be unfulfilling and wasteful?—some of them relate to fork-in-the-road moments from years, even decades earlier in my life. And while I know there's little point in looping back over the same well-tread mental territory, that doesn't always allow me to drop the issue and nudge my focus back toward the more meaningful, controllable present.

All of us will have different relationships with regret, but there's some evidence that the modern world, with its ever-inflating abundance of options, sparks more regretful moments than previous periods because there's simply more opportunity to make choices that go awry.

There's also reason to believe that, though regret is an internal, self-critical experience, concern that other people might find out about our bad choice, our failure to act, the dumb joke we told, the *faux pas* we committed, or the debts that remain unpaid can amplify our anxiety, converting rumination about our actions into concrete fears of diminished social standing, and modern communication tools and norms can increase the likelihood of such exposure.

The older we get, the more life we've lived, and the more opportunity we've had to make mistakes and regret our choices.

Some therapists recommend experiencing, amending, forgiving, reframing, and then using regret to improve ourselves and our lives, as a sort of multi-step process for coping with difficult-to-shake regretful moments.

Experiencing, in this context, means acknowledging that something regretful happened, but doing so in a productive, arm's-length manner that allows for immersion without wallowing. Let the memory in, notice and accept what happened, coldly recognize why we respond to that memory the way we do, and then re-shelve it—put it away and out of mind because there's nothing more we can or need to do with it.

It can also be useful to make amends if there's something we can actually do to right a wrong.

For instance, we can try to make monetary amends after knowingly stiffing someone in a deal, or if we said or did something horrible that hurt a friend, we might apologize (if doing so would be likely to help them, rather than pointlessly opening an old wound).

We can also forgive ourselves by recognizing that if someone we cared about was feeling this kind of guilt about something they did to us, we would probably be capable of forgiving them, and we should thus offer ourselves the same grace, assuming we've made amends if warranted and assuming we've learned from the experience (and adjusted our behavior accordingly).

Reframing can help us put regrets into proper context and proportion.

I find it helps to remind myself that I like my life and that I wouldn't have it if anything had gone differently, even the bad stuff.

But it can also be productive to keep in mind that other people probably don't remember the regrettable thing we did the same way we do, if they remember it at all, and that (for instance) we're statistically unlikely to time the stock market and make it big on a specific trade, and that attempting to do so is more likely to lose us money than earn us anything; according to the odds, then, despite our choice looking less than ideal when viewed through the lens of all-knowing retrospect, we probably made the right decision based on what we knew at the moment, not buying that stock that doubled in value.

Regret can also help us center our attention and refocus on what's meaningful to us, because our agonized fixations often shape our priorities and ethics, which in turn shape our sense of who we should be in the future.

By working through our list of dissatisfactions, item by item, healthfully setting each rueful preoccupation aside and forgiving ourselves after we've addressed it, we can build us-shaped scaffoldings for the selves we'd like to become while also recognizing and appreciating the positive changes we've already made because of earlier efforts.

One more useful idea is that of acceptance: being capable of recognizing what is and what can be, but also what isn't and cannot be, no matter how much we might wish otherwise.

I'm unlikely to be able to afford a luxury yacht anytime soon, and if that was on my list of priorities, I would need to come to terms with the fact that I won't be spending the waning days of my 30s yachting around the world.

I might feel inclined to beat myself up over my lack of yacht-scale financial success, but it's a lot more productive and rational to acknowledge and then accept this reality for what it is. I don't have to be happy about this state of monetary affairs, but I have the choice to either be super-bummed forever about this failure to make something happen, or to decide that I'll make the best of what is: choosing to enjoy the wonderful elements of the life I'm actually living, rather than perceptually diminishing my life by comparing it to a variation that includes more yachting, but which may never have been terribly realistic (or even happiness-inducing, for me) to begin with.

By accepting what is I'm able to make the best of whatever I've got and whatever comes next, and while it's important to not adopt a stance of powerlessness—of assuming that because I'll accept whatever happens, there's no reason to put effort into anything—it's a beneficial skill to hone, being able to find the value in any kind of life.

Ultimately, that we are around to regret our past mistakes and are still alive enough to make new and exciting missteps is something to be celebrated, not something to fixate on to where we cannot appreciate and enjoy our continued, potential-full existence.

Habits

The things we do every day define who we are now and pave the path toward who we become.

Our rituals, routines, and habits, then, shape our lives. They determine how we spend our time, what outcomes we can expect (immediately and eventually), and they orient us toward our goals, helping us focus on those ultimate destinations despite life's myriad (and potent) distractions.

Some of my most practical and valuable habits are the simplest.

I drink water throughout the day, for instance, and maintain my intake by keeping a giant vacuum-walled tumbler at my desk (or wherever else I'm working).

I also do a little 20-minute workout first thing each morning, brush my teeth and wash my face before going to sleep each night, and do crossword and sudoku puzzles after lunch, before getting back to work.

These are small, even trifling habits, but routine (even low-key) maintenance of our bodies and minds can avert issues that might otherwise accumulate.

Many of my other habits, like taking the stairs when possible, practical, and advisable, and reading fiction before going to sleep, are likewise simple and unobtrusive, but they're also helpful and healthful in outsized proportion to the effort they require.

Habits needn't be cumbersome or draining to be useful. Some will be, but many of the most valuable ones frictionlessly slide right into our lives. Genuine effort might be required when we're initially locking a new habit into place and making sure it sticks, but it will be easier to maintain after that initial investment.

Habits can also be more periodic, triggering only when they're needed, like reflexes, rather than activating on a predictable schedule.

I love being alone, and I crave solitude and privacy when I'm around other people for too long. But I know from experience that after living with someone for a while, I can suffer something close to a minor panic attack when I'm suddenly alone for a long period.

After a day or two, I'm back to enjoying my solitude, sinking into a comforting, me-shaped routine. But for those first few days, I may have to fend off an intermittent procession of little psychological jolts that make me feel isolated, separated from the world, and lonely.

I've learned that in these moments it's best to take a walk, go to the store, or do something else that allows me to be around people without actively forcing other humans to keep me company. That helps me ease from one norm to the other with a minimum of fuss and suffering.

When I'm stressing about something work-related or some kind of social conflict, being around animals and nature—taking a walk through the park or petting a stranger's dog—helps a lot.

When I'm feeling low on energy and a bit glum, working out (almost any kind of exercise, but something involving cardio works particularly well) perks me back up.

These are things I've had to learn with time, and this type of personal knowledge becomes more accessible the older we get, provided we pay attention and view our behaviors and responses as components of a larger pattern (rather than issues we should slapdashedly salve and move past as quickly as possible).

Most of us develop custom habitual tools that become more potent and surgical with age because we've been through enough and know enough about ourselves and other people to dream up remedies that are suitable for a given ailment—our likelihood of success increasing with each passing year, as long as we pay attention and continue to refine these tools.

We show (and remind) ourselves who we are through all the little things we do.

Taking care of the dishes in the sink rather than letting them sit and accumulate is one way of showing ourselves that we're motivated and on the ball, doing things that need to be done, now, rather than waiting till "someday." Internalizing this perception can then carry over into the decisions we make (and the effort we exert) across the other aspects of our lives.

The reflexes we choose to develop also demonstrate something about who we are, what we care about, and where we're headed.

Investing energy and effort to better understand what causes what, what triggers make us feel which way, and to iterate solutions that help us be the version of ourselves we'd like to be (more of the time), reinforces the internal sense that we have control over what we do, how we do it, and who we are as individuals as we go about our business.

It can take a while to build up this perception, and it can take still-longer for these sorts of habits to stick. But minor acts over time accumulate into something larger than the sum of their parts, while also serving as fuel for future, beneficial action.

Beginnings

While it's vital we learn to uproot things from our lives that aren't serving us—things that stand between us and what we hope to accomplish, how we'd like to feel, and the growth we're keen to stoke—it's also important that we can intentionally start new things, as otherwise we're prone to leaving unwanted gaps in our lives, or replacing one ill-fitting habit or system or relationship (or whatever else) with another.

Rather than passively accepting whatever routines, connections, or ambitions are readily at hand, it's often more productive to carefully and intentionally sort through our options, to identify those that aren't casually available (but which we would like to pursue), and to then work through the process of incorporating them into our lives.

Which a fancy way of saying we should do things on purpose, rather than allowing ourselves to be blown around by the winds of happenstance.

This is especially important when we're starting something new, whether that's a new life in an unfamiliar town, a new partnership, or a fresh start at the dawn of a new year, as it can seem intuitive to fill perceptual voids in our lives with whatever we can easily grab. Mapping what we hope to accomplish and plotting out how we might take steps in that direction, though, is more effective than frantically adopting whatever's available, giving little thought to how an uninterrogated deviation might affect our ambitions.

Beginnings are opportunities to lay the groundwork for future efforts and to implement changes because there's less existing infrastructure and fewer expectations to compete with as we move in a new, more optimal direction.

It's possible to make a hard segue toward a novel endpoint any time we choose, but attempting to pivot while juggling the responsibilities and rewards of the current paradigm can be an unnecessarily cumbersome undertaking.

Thus, when something new is impending or something old is ending, that's an ideal moment to plant the seeds we want to plant and to reorganize everything so that we're more likely to end up with our desired outcome, as there will be less struggle, fewer antique systems and habits to compete with, and we'll suffer fewer loss-aversion-related pangs as we turn toward something more us-shaped.

Variables beyond our control will sometimes serendipitously shift fate in our favor, paving some of the path toward our existing ambitions, or shining a spotlight on outcomes we hadn't considered, but which, now illuminated, are obviously desirable and freshly within reach.

There will also be moments in which that's what seems to be happening, but in reality our brains are trying to convince us to settle for something convenient (and less energy-intensive), and the airy accomplishment on offer would be a mere shadow of what we'd actually like to pursue.

Such perfunctory (though tempting) paths usually lead back to where we started: unhappy with what we've got and longing to progress toward something better.

It's almost always more ideal to attempt the richer, deeper, denser goal, even if it'll take longer to achieve, and even if our brains try to dissuade us by pointing out easier options and reminding us of how stressful it can be to chase something we might never catch, and to expose ourselves to potential failure.

We have more opportunities to start things as we get older both because we've lived longer and because we've survived more extrinsic paradigm shifts (changes in technology, politics, relationships, etc) that can serve as catalysts for our own internal tweaks, if we choose to act on them.

Any time we like, we can uproot the aspects of our lives that aren't working, till the now-vacant soil, and then plant something that better serves our purposes. But it's often easier, psychologically and sociologically, to do so during milestone moments, and the longer we live, the more such moments we enjoy.

Use or Lose

There's evidence that although our sense of smell diminishes as we age, it's possible to intentionally use this sense so that we maintain our youthful capacity, maybe even enhancing our olfactory powers as we grow older.

This same general concept applies to just about everything we might lose as we age, from our memory to our cognitive potency to our muscles and bones and aptitude for building and maintaining and enjoying relationships.

We derive benefits from picking up a pair of dumbbells and joining a cycling class even after decades of not exercising, but it's wiser to commit to maintaining one's body and mind and skills than to set them aside for ages, dusting off the accumulated cobwebs years later and hoping everything still works as intended.

While not being used, our capabilities and competencies rust and wear, accruing flaws that might not be fixable no matter how much we need (and miss) them, and how diligent our attempts at repair and polish.

It also becomes a lot more difficult to pull oneself back into the rhythm of (for instance) running or doing daily crossword puzzles after swinging hard in the opposite direction, going without for long periods of time.

The muscles we develop for such efforts (literal and figurative) atrophy, and our psychological capacity to do difficult things, to grit our teeth and work through the pain and discomfort, to make cognitive investments, wondering throughout if we might be unequal to the task, diminishes with disuse.

Part of the difficulty is that many of us don't have habits or rituals or routines oriented around strengthening or maintaining our brains, bodies, and skills even when we're young, because many of these things are easier when the relevant bodily components are fresh off the assembly line.

There isn't a moment in which someone pulls us aside and says, "Okay, everything will be a bit more difficult from this point forward, and a lot more difficult after that," so the transition from "everything's easy" to "everything's harder" leaves us scant opportunity to bulwark ourselves against those impending changes, developing suitable maintenance procedures and reinforcing our most vulnerable elements.

Had we such a moment, we'd be better prepared to counter these issues before they become significant headaches. But because we don't, many of us only think about them after they've become tangible, life-altering burdens: we do crosswords because we heard it might help with the memory challenges we now face, or we take up yoga because of the persistent hip pain we've been suffering.

The more we can do to get ahead of these impending adversities, the better. Preempting them allows us to fix problems before they become problems, to erect the scaffolding for our next-step, self-sustaining rhythms, and it helps us blunt or prevent the worst-case, permanent downsides of neglecting fundamental (but not invulnerable) components of ourselves for too long.

Empowered

One way we might think about aging is through the lens of empowerment.

Ideally, each year we increase the number of life components over which we feel we have power, and over which we actually do.

This will mean different things for different people and different facets of our lives, but we might decide that we're going to figure out how to manage our own finances, or that we're going to learn how to take better care of our skin.

The idea is to shore up weak spots we already know we have, while also keeping watch for other elements (internal or external) that we might want to oversee more intentionally—even if we're not sure what that will entail, at first.

Empowerment is a double-edged sword, as taking control of something also means taking responsibility for it. This represents an opportunity to fail, but also a chance to right-size and prioritize things that aren't currently receiving the attention and energy they deserve, while relegating others to a more minor role, even if they've previously received significant consideration.

Grabbing hold of the reins in this way requires both education and self-knowledge, necessitating that we (for instance) research the best financial investments for our age, priorities, and monetary circumstances, while also doing the internal work required to determine what our priorities actually are and how we might rearrange other dimensions of our lives (like our careers or our spending habits) to give ourselves more options as we attempt to bring order to our pocketbooks and bank accounts.

I enjoy thinking about aging in this way, because although it can sometimes be stressful to tally the vast number of things over which I (currently) have less control than I might like, this way of thinking also serves as a reminder that I've been gradually wrangling authority over more dimensions of my life since I've been old enough to feed myself and putter around the house on my own, and it feels good to recognize my efforts and notice the positive things that have resulted from many of them.

It's also nice to think about my next chronological steps as opportunities to further refine my life: each new day laden with potential, and that potential broadening as I earn more agency over a larger portion of what makes me, me.

Becoming Old

I only came to appreciate what it feels like to be old after aging into the latter-half of my 30s.

This isn't an omnipresent thing: there are still contexts in which I'm obviously the youngest person in the room. But now I'm regularly the old guy in a discussion or at an event, and there are an increasing number of things that are ostensibly "not for me" in the collective cultural consciousness.

That latter point is important to the experience of feeling older, I think. Much of mainstream culture, in many societies, orients around an adulation of and fixation on youth and youthfulness.

After you age past a certain point, literally or perceptually, you're no longer in that target demographic, and you no longer benefit (and suffer) from its rewards and burdens, which include, among other things, persistent surveillance of your behaviors and preferences, pervasive celebration and sexualization of everything you are and seem to be, and a concomitant cacophony of concern about who and what you will become, filtered through the lens of earlier generational norms and standards.

Older people, from time immemorial, have worried about the future, that future shaped by young people who are themselves shaped by variables older folks don't fully understand: different economic conditions, different bodies of knowledge, different pop cultures and influential personalities, and countless others.

We are a species that incessantly mourns norms that are on their way out or that we've already cast aside, and we harbor untold anxieties about what comes next because each era's fresh batch of youths seems primed to lead humanity down a well-paved path toward destruction.

That destruction hasn't happened yet, and it's likely all such concerns, past, present, and future, have more to do with those older generations feeling elbowed out by clutches of young people who are now the center of attention, all their familiar folkways back-burnered in favor of the new hotness, than any real, concrete societal unease.

Experiencing this transition from spotlighted youth to shadow-dwelling adult has been interesting, in part because there have been moments in which I've felt completely left out of a novel trend or other social development, and have had to remind myself that this thing isn't inherently bad or harmful, it's just not for me. And because it's not for me, I may not be in the position to understand it (or fully grok it if I manage to attain a basic understanding).

This, to me, is both a benefit and a downside of getting older, as I no longer feel compelled to be part of (or even aware of) all these new happenings, many of which will be momentary blips that no one remembers a few weeks after their pop cultural apex, and that means I can be more selective about where I invest my finite time, energy, and resources.

Existing outside that spotlight also means we can revisit, revise, and even reinvent ourselves without being monitored by the ever-present forces of youth-scrutiny.

Different people have different standards applied to them, and society slaps a boggling number of additional expectations on women in particular. But the common assumption that part of a young person's value is aesthetic, and the rest is based on their potential (what they'll do in the future, not what they're doing or capable of doing now), whatever their individual traits, can lead to self-diminishment, motivating us to reshape our lives, actions, and priorities so they fit within those externally implemented constraints. That leaves us with fewer perceptually legitimate life paths, most of which won't line up with how we'd like to do things and where we'd like to go.

Stepping beyond that spotlight—or more commonly, I think, having the spotlight deviate away from us without our realizing what's happening—can be liberating, then, as the expectations and faculties of an adult are different, and if we wield these powers appropriately, we enjoy a greater number of socially acceptable paths to choose from, alongside our new capacity to blaze our own trails without suffering the penalties imposed on misbehaving, norm-defying youths.

We face social expectations and limitations at every age, but the grading criteria changes as we grow older, and that broadly allows for more freedom of movement and experimentation.

The more aged we become, too, the more likely we are to be seen as a whole person who's doing things on purpose, rather than an incomplete, wayward youth who doesn't yet understand how the world works, and who is consequently acting almost entirely based on instinct and ignorance (warranting correction from wise elders who know better).

There are plenty of downsides to growing older, including seemingly causeless body aches, a higher likelihood of previously benign genetic issues popping up, and a cluster of extra responsibilities and expectations related to family and work and finances.

We also tend to become less open to new experiences after age 50 (or thereabouts), our cognitive powers reorient away from flashy, impressive feats of processing, and our memories begin to deteriorate. A slew of disconcerting and disorienting reallocations of bodily resources can cause fat and muscle to accumulate differently, our hair to thin and fall out, and our previously familiar and regular drives and rhythms (sleep, sex, diet) to change cadence or disappear entirely.

But on the plus side, we're freed from many suffocating social expectations, which means we can choose to participate in previously vital elements of social discourse, or decide not to.

We become more confident, more secure (in ourselves, but usually financially and structurally, as well), and we generally enjoy greater self-understanding and a more refined sense of self-in-context, which can make it easier to wrestle with difficult philosophical and spiritual questions.

We, on average, benefit from a more consistent positive affect—an optimistic, upbeat, and agreeable outlook on things—as we grow older, and it becomes easier to ignore the negative stuff, as we know from experience that those feelings are temporary, and the bad stuff diminishes as we recall, adjust, and re-shelf those memories over and over again, usually from a place of greater fulfillment and self-certitude; the bad slowly filtered away and replaced with good.

We also become less neurotic and envious as we grow older, and though this will vary from person to person like everything else, this change seems to be at least partially the consequence of our extraction from the spotlight, which reduces our knee-jerk need to perform and compete in a psychologically draining way.

Aging isn't easy, and it's not straightforward, either. It's not just one thing that changes, and it doesn't change along a straight line, or the same way for every person or within every cultural context.

Growing older in the biological sense, in the self-perception sense, and in the sense that other people perceive us to be older, though, seems to influence a huge number of variables that shape many aspects of our lives. While some of these changes are difficult and even painful to face, others are a relief: a breath of fresh air after an initial few decades burdened with (arguably unjust) expectations, pressures, and constraints.

Forgiveness

We've all done things we wish we hadn't done.

We've all lived through moments we wish had turned out another way.

We've all been wronged and wronged others, intentionally or neglectfully, consciously or completely ignorant of our trespass until years later when, in a moment of dot-connecting, we realize we were bad, caused harm, acted against our sense of moral correctness, and then kept right on living our lives as if nothing had happened (a luxury not afforded to those on the other end of our actions).

Time passes and with each new day comes a fresh opportunity to let go of grudges, of resentments, of quarrels, vengefulness, animosity, and self-reproach.

"Rumination" refers to a cycle of purposeless negative thinking, powered by our sense of regret and assumed regret, that can sprawl across the whole of our lives if we don't halt it.

It's worth understanding that, although something in our minds might insist an event, a concern, a memory should remain at the forefront of our attention, that doesn't mean it's important: not everything is a lesson, sometimes things just happen.

Some things are lessons, though, and one way to hit the brakes on that rumination cycle is to wring what value we can from experiences that get stuck and won't shake loose. Thinking such things through, figuring out what we might glean from them, and then implementing that new wisdom to the best of our ability can sometimes help us more forward.

Whether we find a particular rumination to be pointless or pointed, though, going through the process of clear-eyed assessment earns us the ability to set these thoughts aside and relegate them to a category of regrettable, but not overwhelming and life-defining memories.

In this way, we can consciously and intentionally forgive ourselves, acting upon the actionable and accepting the things we can't do anything about.

We have the power to forgive others, as well, and in doing so, we free ourselves of the psychological burden of maintaining that animosity and clinging to a cumbersome sense of being wronged.

We get to decide what's important and what's not, what we take as an insult or injury, and what we laugh off, forget, or excuse.

Forgiveness is a superpower we can choose to wield. As we grow older and our capacity for conscientiousness and our diversity of experiences (and consequent wisdom) grows, it can be easier to leverage this power for productive purposes, shrugging off inherited ideas about grudges and revenge, and choosing (more of the time, at least) to leave such millstones in our past, demonstrating our strength through our ability to set unnecessary burdens aside, rather than showing off how much we can carry.

Memory

Although we have a general sense of how memory works, we've yet to prove our dominant theories, and we're all different in how we capture, process, store, and summon brain-logged information, so even a more concrete understanding of the neurological underpinnings of memory won't tell us everything we want to know about it for personal application.

What many researchers think, though, is that we jot down what we experience in our short-term memory, in metaphorical pencil, and then eventually incorporate some of those temporary jottings into long-term storage based on variables like how often we reference a particular note or how much emotional or sensory metadata we've attached to it.

Something I find useful to keep in mind about memory, especially as I get older and accumulate more noteworthy moments and knowledge I'd like to tuck away, is that our remembering systems are imperfect and become even more so the older we get, and the more distance we put between ourselves and whatever we're recalling.

We filter our memories through the lenses of bias and prejudice and presumption, alongside those related to variables like where we were standing when something happened. Our brain mechanisms fill in blanks when we don't have enough data to really know what went down, and these blank-filling tendencies are great when we need to make predictions and assumptions that may help us survive, but not so wonderful when we're trying to understand (for instance) who was at fault in a car accident or who said what during an emotionally charged argument with a partner.

From the get-go, then, the memory data we save and revisit is flawed in the sense that it doesn't represent objective truth; it's subjective sensory information that's warped until it aligns with our understanding of the world, any blank spaces filled with completely fabricated details that seem real and help us imagine a more cohesive and comprehensible (to us) whole.

When we recall a memory, it's a bit like pulling a book from a shelf: we touch the book, the oils from our fingers seeping into the cover. We turn the pages, which with time accumulate little tears and folds and creases.

Over the years, even with careful handling, these mental-books wear into new shapes, and there's evidence that our state of mind when we revisit them can influence the shape they take.

So if we revisit a memory of a teenage breakup from a moment of comparable calm and happiness when we're in our 30s, that can nudge a memory tinged with tumult and emotional difficulty into a more stable, accepting, peaceful state.

This is also, by the way, why it's sometimes possible to diminish the impact of traumatic memories (even of PTSD-level events) by regularly and intentionally revisiting them in safe, calming environments. Over time, we can layer these memories with additional, context-derived metadata that smooths their spiky bits, allowing us to handle them safely in the future.

Engaging with our memories can thus distort and filter them so they seem worse, better, or more or less important than they were. We can even come to remember things that didn't happen, especially if someone repeatedly shares a narrative of something that differs from our memory of the same. Over time, our brains may integrate their oft-recounted version of events, and we may come to truly believe their version is what actually happened, because our memory data will have been subtly but permanently altered by all those revisitations.

We're also prone to memory biases, better recalling things that stand out than things that align with norms and expectations, for instance, and recalling things that are meaningful to what we've been thinking about with greater clarity than things that are outside our conscious ken.

We remember things that happened recently better than things that were more important or impactful, but which happened a long while ago, because older memories become less well-defined as we pile fresh memories (even mundane ones) onto the chronological stack.

Owning an overall larger collection of memories can also distort our perception.

At the cusp of 40, I already sometimes have trouble summoning details from my childhood and early adulthood because I've lived so much life since I originally archived those memories. The highlights stand out, as do moments that are often revisited or retold by friends and family, but I have to dig deep and think hard to remember normal, everyday specifics because the things I've done and places I've been and memories I've accumulated in the meantime are more prominent in my archival heap.

It's possible to reengage with memories methodically, though I find it helps to have contemporaneous documentation from the time in question, as otherwise it's impossible to know how much of what we're recalling actually happened, and which parts originate with outside sources, our own biases, or simple errors in mental transcription.

Keeping a journal is one way to do this, and taking photos along the way can help, too.

Reading back over my journal entries at the end of each year helps me establish a more accurate rundown of what occurred in the previous year than my memory, alone, which flattens things and doesn't latently provide with me a sense of temporal context. A lot can happen and be forgotten in a single year, and we can lose meaningful moments in the shuffle if we don't weave these events into the grander, big-picture story periodically.

It's important to balance living our lives with documenting the same, though, because it's possible to take photos of experiences instead of actually experiencing them, perceiving the world through the lenses of our cameras, and to spend more time mulling over what's happened than engaging with the world of today—which does our future selves, who will only have what memories we collect and preserve for them, a disservice.

Accomplishment

As we grow older and step into new phases of life, our earlier goals and metrics for success may no longer apply, or no longer apply in the same way.

Segueing from an academic career into a job can be tricky, for instance, because the things that made us successful in school won't directly map onto work-world success.

Similarly, retiring can be disorienting because many of us at least partly define ourselves through the lens of our jobs and careers, and if we no longer shoulder that money-earning burden, who even are we?

No matter how much we have accomplished in work, in our family life, in our hobbies or volunteering or whatever else, the perception of not having done enough—or maybe we should have done things differently?—can amplify this disorientation.

When we're younger, this feeling is non-ideal, but it's not the end of the world because we have plenty of time (perceptually at least) to fill in any gaps that gnaw at us.

The older we get, though, the less time we have left. Every day lived marks another day closer to death, and a little more time behind us than ahead of us.

Though life once felt infinite and we walked the earth as immortals, dawdling away our bottomless chronologies, that sense of near-boredom eventually becomes a bone-deep awareness of our own finitude, alongside a worry that there's no way we'll be able to cram everything we'd like to do into the seemingly scarce existence we have left.

This is silly, of course: the average middle-aged person living in the modern world has decades of life left to enjoy. But it doesn't feel silly, and the changes we experience to our minds and bodies shape a lot of what we do in the latter half of our lives, nudging us toward triage-like decisions rather than calm, intentional investments in the things that really matter to us.

We're also more capable of achieving some goals in our later years than in our youths because of our accumulated wisdom, knowledge, and experience, and because we'll likely have access to more resources and will be in a better position to use them appropriately (rather than thoughtlessly throwing everything we've got at said goals, youthfully assuming that if our ham-handed efforts fail, we'll have enough time to bounce back and try again).

There are a few accomplishment-related things I've been trying to keep in mind as I grow older.

First is that it's important to know what we actually want, and to distinguish those wants from mimetic and inherited wants. This means figuring out when a desire is intrinsic and us-centered, and when a want is actually the consequence of other people wanting something, or being told (perhaps in our formative years) that we should want something, and then treating that extrinsic aspiration as if it were our own.

It's also important to have an accurate sense of what "enough" means in different facets of our lives, because without a ceiling on that concept we may waste some or all of our time, energy, and resources on (for instance) accumulating more money than we need or attaining the pinnacle of professional prestige, when a smaller bank account and lower-level position would have better served our true needs and wants, freeing up our finite resources for other pursuits.

This is important because without that self-defined, self-optimized ceiling, a single aspect of our lives can drain us of the capacity to invest in other aspects, appropriately, and that can flatten us into one-dimensional versions of ourselves. It can also make it less likely we'll ever step away from that mono-focus until much later in our lives, because self-protective biases like loss aversion will try to dissuade us from cutting our losses (even when it's prudent to do so), and because we may never take or have the time to step back and ask ourselves whether we're doing what we want to be doing.

Second is that our sense of what's vital, what's pointless, and what's nice-to-have (but not fundamental to our happiness) all change as we change, so it's important to check in on these assumptions periodically, lest we continue to perform familiar routines but enjoy fewer meaningful benefits over time, not noticing the diminishment because the rhythms and habits have become so ingrained in our lives and minds.

Third is that it's helpful to acknowledge and take stock of what we experience as regret, but to remind ourselves that there are often good reasons we didn't accomplish something, and many times those tradeoffs were worthwhile, even if we may wonder and worry, coveting the greener grass on the other side of the potentiality fence because we experience the downsides of the path we took, daily, but we can only see the desirable upsides, all the stuff we didn't get, from the path we didn't take.

Regrets can be useful because the painful pangs they cause can help us reorient ourselves, helping us do more of the things that will fulfill us (rather than less important stuff) in the future. But they're also often predicated on ill-informed gut-feelings, and we can experience them even after they're no longer relevant (when we no longer want the things to which they apply). It's important we take what we can from regrets, then, but that we don't develop a habit of wallowing in them without productive purpose.

Finally, it's helpful to incorporate more "atelic" activities (those without defined end-points or concrete goals) into our lives to temper the "telic" ones (those with definitive cut-offs and outcomes) as we grow older.

This helps us become accustomed to doing things just to do them, enjoying the journey and not living exclusively for the destination, and it can help us define ourselves in non-accomplishment-oriented terms.

Many of us find it difficult to do this, especially in a world where our perceived value is largely determined by our economic activity. Incorporating stuff we do for fun, stuff we do while staying in the moment, and stuff that's just exploratory and experimental (rather than focused on a fixed outcome and end-date), then, can help us chisel new facets into our sense of self, rounding us out while making us less reliant on attainments of a monetizable, socially celebrated, often age-bracketed variety.

Money

Money isn't everything, but it is something.

That'll remain true unless the world in which we live fundamentally changes, which isn't impossible, but it's also not something we should bet on for the foreseeable future.

That in mind, while everyone's financial situation is unique, it's generally prudent to spend less than we make, acquire more assets and fewer liabilities over time, invest more in things that actually matter to us and less in things that don't, to save, to accumulate interest on the resources we have, and to develop a healthy relationship with money so we can manage it without obsessing over or stressing about it.

It also helps to establish a ceiling—a sense of what "enough" looks like—so that we know how much of ourselves to exchange for a sum of money.

If we have very little in the bank and not much in the way of income, it may be worth taking a job we hate, temporarily, if it'll net us a guaranteed $35,000 a year. That payout might not be worth the time and psychological energy spent, though, if we're already millionaires (or if we're already doing okay with the relatively little we've got).

Figuring out how much money is enough for us and our priorities is the work of a lifetime, because it's not just a matter of having enough in the bank to pay for our essentials and our wants, it's also about addressing money-related feelings and understandings we inherited as children, establishing a sense of security and control over our lives, and determining how valuable things like our time, energy, and spiritual or ideological fulfillment are so that we don't accidentally trade too much of them away.

I've found it useful to establish a baseline level of spending and earning that allows me to sustain myself and my lifestyle at a functional level, along with a moderate volume of minor luxuries.

Using this standard as a reference point, as my earning and spending minimum, rather than relying on figures given to me by other people or society, I'm able to make more me-shaped financial decisions and avoid over-investing in undertakings that would earn me more money, but which would cost me a lot more than I gain, when also considering non-financial metrics.

Establishing this sort of baseline allows us to be more confident when accepting a new job, starting a business, or deciding to not work at all for a while, even if such choices would mean we're making less money. As long as we're able to meet that low-end, sustained and satisfied figure we computed, we'll still be okay, money-wise, as we spent some time pursuing success of another flavor.

This is not financial advice—we're all different people with different wants, needs, and circumstances—and we therefore all have different upper and lower boundaries for this sort of thing, which means some of us will need more money to pursue fulfillment on our terms, while others will require far less.

Whatever our specifics, though, it's important we invest in our vital non-money metrics (the things we truly care about) even as we do what we can to reinforce our financial weak spots: treating it as something over which we have control, rather than something that sparks stress and anxiety on one end of the spectrum, or which we thoughtlessly obsess over to the exclusion of all else, on the other.

Appreciation and Inspiration

The older we get, the more likely we are to feel excluded from new trends, technologies, and social mores.

This perceived exclusion, paired with our growing experience with past versions of the same (which have long since lapsed in popularity and relevance) can make it difficult to muster enthusiasm for these sorts of (maybe temporal) things.

This conscious or unconscious distancing can be further amplified by commercial entities' persistent refocusing of their attention on the most youthful adult (or nearly adult) generation of the moment, which can make it seem (to us adults) as if the entire world is constantly falling all over itself to flog the dumbest possible things (that we don't get and don't want to get, because these things are stupid and meant for children).

Because of this (often understandable) distancing, we may find ourselves short on inspiration and creative drive, because many of the elements that inform our growth, cognitive expansion, and sense of what's possible are no longer fueling us.

We might replace some of these forces with different versions of the same—spending more time learning about history, for instance—but if we don't consciously try to remain connected to the (ever-evolving) modern world, we may begin to feel peripheral to today's movements, creations, explorations, ideas, innovations, and experiments to the detriment of our understanding of what's happening, why it matters, and where we fit.

None of which is destiny. At any age, we can decide to remain "of the world" rather than pushing away from things that don't make immediate sense to us, and which don't cater to our existing understandings and preferences. But the older we get, the more effort will tend to be necessary to stay connected in this way, and to maintain our capacity for appreciation and inspiration.

I find it's useful to remind myself that there's a difference between appreciating something and liking it.

It's possible, for instance, to listen to a genre of music we don't like, but to still appreciate what the artists are doing or trying to do, and consequently to understand what's "good" according to the metrics specific to that genre, and what's "less successful" according to the same.

This can be a more productive stance than carving up the world into "things I like" and "things I don't like," because it allows us to grasp even things we don't enjoy, which can be satisfying. Not liking something can also flatten our sense of self-definition ("I am the sort of person who doesn't like x"), while understanding, in contrast, renders the question of liking or not liking almost beside the point, and that leaves an opening for potentially growing to like something in the future, while allowing us to keep an open mind (without conflicting with a disliking-oriented self-definition) in the meantime.

I also find the concept of the Illusion of Explanatory Depth helpful when I have a knee-jerk, negative response to something. This illusion gestures at our tendency to believe we know more about something than we actually do, and one way to bypass this bias is to explain the thing we think we know in great detail to someone else.

Most of us would probably reflexively assume we know how a bicycle works. But if we're asked to draw a diagram of a bike and exhaustively explain what all the pieces do and how they fit together, almost all of us would fail spectacularly.

We don't actually understand many of the things we believe we understand, then, potentially including genres of music we deride and cultural trends we think are nonsensical.

Appreciation (when liking isn't in the cards) can fuel our creative and informational inputs with new raw materials and prevent the deployment of a dislike filter that keeps anything interesting from getting in. It can also remind us to not automatically distance ourselves from people and trends that don't superficially align with our existing preferences, desires, and understandings.

Maintenance

The Red Queen Hypothesis asserts that organisms must evolve rapidly to stay competitive with their ever-strengthening (and speedier and more clever) predators, prey, and peer species.

This term originates with the Red Queen character in the book *Through the Looking Glass, and What Alice Found There* (the sequel to *Alice's Adventures in Wonderland*), who explains to Alice that in her world everyone must run faster and faster just to stay where they are, to avoid falling behind.

Experts have also applied this concept to fields like business and fraud detection: areas in which competition is stiff and individuals must always be moving to maintain their current state, status, or position.

I would argue it also applies to aging, as elements of our bodies and brains are always changing, and the more years we accumulate, the more maintenance we must do just to keep things operating at roughly the same baseline.

As we enter our 40s and 50s, for instance, the number of taste buds in our mouths decreases and the buds that remain shrink, a process we experience as a diminishment in our capacity to taste.

Our sense of smell weakens in our 60s, and because smell is a component of taste, our flavor-detecting capacity is further reduced.

That said, there's evidence that intentionally using these senses—not just picking up on random odors and flavors, but consciously indulging in taste-testing and smell-seeking, engaging with a variety of fragrances and foods—can help us maintain both our receptors and the connections between these receptors and the parts of our brains that interpret their signals.

Similarly, using our muscles, our tendons and ligaments, our balance and flexibility and kinesthetic sense of self-in-space can help us maintain these bodily components and capacities.

This "use it or lose it" concept is easy to understand, but it's difficult to plan and perform the routines that are necessary to sustain all the things we would like to keep from degrading and withering away. There are only so many hours in the day, and while it may seem simple enough to introduce more food- and wine-tastings, perfume- and flower-smelling activities into our lives, they're all competing for time, energy, and resources with every other thing we'd like to do, including all the other maintenance tasks we set for ourselves.

And there are potentially many of them!

As we age, some activities and relationships—friendships and romantic partners, daily crossword puzzles and reading a book before bed—might be effortless to uphold because these are things we enjoy doing, and we may already have habits that root them in our rhythms.

But what about a daily workout routine for those of us who don't already have one, and who don't particularly enjoy weight-lifting, yoga-ing, or stretching our (tense, tight) hamstrings?

What about maintaining a sense of what's happening in the world, soaking up enough news and knowledge to maintain our situational awareness, but not so much that it overwhelms or negatively affects our psyches?

How about maintaining the capacity for growth in an ever-changing personal and global context? Even something as simple as keeping up with music requires we spend time (which we otherwise might expend consciously smelling perfumes or exercising) sampling enough of what's out there so that we understand our options and can discover recent artists and albums we might enjoy.

Each of these efforts are investments that potentially pay substantial dividends, and just as we can benefit from compounding interest by strategically investing our money over time, we can also benefit from maintaining aspects of our lives and health, and the sooner we start, the better.

As with monetary investments, though, there are finite resources to spread around, so the challenge is figuring out what to prioritize.

I try to think about this as an exercise in optimization, prominence, and urgency.

When optimizing our maintenance efforts, we may discover ways to blend some of our tasks with other tasks, or to make them seem less effortful by reformulating them into enjoyable activities.

We can go on wine-tasting and perfume-smelling excursions with our partners, and we can engage in hobbies we'd like to maintain with friends who have similar interests (new music listening nights, spinning classes at the gym, and so on).

It's also possible to rank this array of potential efforts based on what we think will be most vital to our future selves who will benefit (or suffer) from the choices we make.

Some age-degrading aspects of our lives, like physical movement and memory, will be pretty universal in terms of future-us appreciating our contemporary maintenance efforts, but other potential targets won't be as obvious, at first.

Thinking it through, though, we may realize that maintaining our eyesight is actually pretty vital to our enjoyment of life, or that losing the capacity to play catch with our grandkids might be a really hard pill to swallow, so these would be things to start working on as soon as possible, addressing other, less-pressing matters later.

Depending on our age and circumstances, some of these attributes might be disappearing already, and it may thus be prudent to establish maintenance habits for those senses, muscle groups, or capacities first; though ideally, we use those initial indicators as reminders that a more holistic maintenance plan is both a prudent and time-sensitive investment.

Transcendence

The term "transcendent" can apply to a boggling array of experiences, and it will mean something slightly different to each of us. But a transcendent experience, in general terms, is something that pulls us out of our familiar modes of thinking and being, extracting us from our usual perspectives and either passing us through or plopping us down into something else entirely.

Some studies have shown that these experiences can help people dealing with PTSD, depression, anxiety, and similar conditions, while also increasing the experiencer's self-reported levels of happiness and awe, and upping the number of stress-free hours they enjoy each day.

People practicing various modalities of meditation, doing breath-work, and engaging in other sorts of body- and mind-state alteration, and those engaging in risky behaviors like sky-diving and high-focus, challenging activities that put us into a state of flow, have reported the same.

There are many ways to nudge (or catapult) ourselves into such a state, and the most common methods of intentionally instigating a sense of transcendence have historically involved religious rituals or psychedelic substances, and practitioners often pair these two catalysts to potent effect.

Spiritual rites like communal dances, the symbolic consumption of flesh, and being blessed by a perceived holy person have a long history of helping people see things, feel things, and experience things that pull back the veil of reality in some ineffable fashion. This has been useful as a curative for maladies, for unifying people around a common cause, and for making people feel a connection with each other—even those with whom they might otherwise not feel connected, or toward whom they might feel the opposite.

Likewise, the use of substances that chemically alter us, changing our perceptual faculties from within, has a long tradition in cultures around the world and throughout time. But it's possible to achieve a similar mind-state via other paths as well, including activities that are significantly more grounded, but no less life-altering and perspective-adjusting.

Having children, for instance, motivates many new parents (after they've had the chance to catch up on sleep) to reassess their lives, what they care about, and how they intend to spend the budget of time they have left on earth.

Becoming a parent, biologically or via adoption, connects us to the future through our children, which expands the scope of chronology that seems relevant and worth working into our concerns and plans, while also putting into perspective all the things we've been focusing on and working toward up to that point, some of which won't seem all that important compared to this new task we've taken on, and this new jumble of concerns that now occupy our time and energy.

Many people also find joining causes to be transcendent in the sense that it allows us to be part of something larger than ourselves, and consequently expands our radius of involvement and concern beyond the confines of a single human being's physical manifestation and lifespan.

Deciding to enter politics or to provide housing for those without shelter or to ensure that kids around the world have access to fundamental levels of education, then, can serve similar purposes as religion, psychedelics, or parenthood, expanding our horizons beyond the reach of our physical forms. They also connect us to other human beings (and their concerns and experiences), and that allows us to glimpse something even bigger.

There's a spectrum of transcendence, some such experiences potent to where we completely lose ourselves, even though they only last a few minutes or hours (tripping on LSD, for instance), while others will be more of a slow-burning segue that lasts years or decades (having a kid and watching them grow, perhaps), recalibrating our compasses in a more ponderous, less dramatic fashion.

Semi-regular encounters with the transcendent seem to be associated with positive psychological outcomes, like dealing with stress more effectively and coping with loss more healthily. Such encounters also seem to make us less self-centered, in the sense that we become more generous, open, and cooperative (though a lot of this research is difficult to dissociate from research related to exposure to any sort of awe, so take these specific claims with a grain of salt).

Most of us would probably benefit from regular exposure to some flavor of transcendence, though, and while there's no reason to think we can't make it through relying purely on worldly outcomes and a full, undissolved sense of self, there seem to be benefits (psychological and community-related) to experimenting with such activities and endeavors, even if the benefits we glean are moderate, or don't pay off until later in our lives.

Stability and Security

I never really appreciated insurance until I hit my 30s.

I would sometimes pay a bit more to increase the scope and span of the warranty on my most vital electronics, and I've always been required by law to have some level of insurance for my car. But for a long time I didn't have health insurance, dental, or anything above and beyond the bare-minimum that was required to maintain foundational (and legal) functionality.

Part of the reasoning here was that I was traveling internationally for most of my 20s and into my mid-30s, so any insurance I might pay for in my home country (the US) would be a sunk investment. I typically had access to some kind of state-provided medical assistance where I lived, and if not, I would pay out-of-pocket for treatment or medicine at a walk-in clinic or similar facility.

But this stance was also a reflection of my sense of invincibility: I had already survived a few near-death experiences by my mid-20s and felt that if something happened to me—something big and life-changing and expensive—I'd cross that bridge when I came to it, rather than throwing my (very finite) monetary resources at problems that may never emerge.

Shortly after entering my 30s, though, an array of new health issues began to plague me, including an autoimmune disease and a series of possibly related (but maybe just stress- and anxiety-induced) scares that necessitated a battery of invasive tests and treatments.

I am still fortunate in this regard; even the most significant and scary health issues I've dealt with have been nothing compared to what many people face throughout their lives.

That said, this was a rather alarming way to step into the latter-half of my 30s, and though nothing truly horrible happened to me, this process of investigation and eventual diagnosis would have been far more burdensome, likely with worse medical and economic outcomes, had I not had health insurance when all this nonsense landed on me out of nowhere.

One of many incredible bummers associated with aging is that although we're more capable and resilient and potent with each passing year (up till the point where everything really falls apart, anyway), we also begin to experience death by a thousand paper cuts sometime around our third decade, as that's when our biological systems have essentially finished up with their prime, procreationary purpose; so from there we're mostly just coasting on fumes.

As we age, then, we face more risks because the corporeal deck is (increasingly) stacked against us.

While anyone can suffer from sickness or genetic mistranscription or random misfortune at any moment and at any age, we're more prone to such things the older we get because our internal systems are no longer actively revivifying themselves. We're thus hit harder by the fists of fate: the bruises lasting longer, the muscles needing more time to mend, our somatic systems (which previously served us so well) only grudgingly helping us out, and even then doing a ham-handed job of it much of the time.

We also have more to lose as we pile on the years, both in the sense that we're more developed, experienced, knowledgeable versions of ourselves (and we therefore have more connections, memories, information, and perspectives we might share with the world), but also in the sense that we'll tend to have more assets and other things we care about than when we were younger.

In our latter years, we've had more time to accumulate all the things humans accumulate, in other words, and that means while there might have been a moment in our youths where we could lose the totality of our possessions and then recoup our losses relatively simply and inexpensively, at some point that's no longer the case. Not only do we have nice stuff and valuable assets to protect, we also have items of personal or spiritual significance, we have responsibilities to other people, pets, and causes, and we're more likely to have carved out niches in society (be it our nation or our neighborhood) that would not be easy to fill were we to disappear from that community because of injury or death.

This is why, as I've gotten older, I've accrued not just more substantial health insurance (which, I should note, is a significant investment here in the US) but also things like AAA (in case my car breaks down) and even dental insurance (which is barely worth having in this country), in case something tragic befalls either me or some vital piece of my personal infrastructure.

I'm enrobed in protective measures meant to dampen the impact of any horribleness that arises, and I expect this category of investment to increase the older I get, even as I do what I can to bulwark my health and car and everything else against misfortune by working out and eating well, changing my oil regularly, and otherwise attempting to stack the deck for positive outcomes on the front end.

These investments are partly practical, but they're also, I suspect, tied to my personal sense of security and stability.

While once I was comfortable wandering the world without backups, confident my Plan A would always work out (and that if it didn't, I'd just suffer my way through the consequences), I've found having a Plan B and C and even D helps me feel more sure of my footing as aspects of my life become less certain because of age-related variables.

I'm proactively doing what I can to keep things from falling apart, then, but I'm also bulwarking my backups, as the likelihood that I'll need them increases with each year.

Different people will have different senses of such things, and I imagine this is especially true for folks who live in countries with better social safety nets (and who are consequently less likely to fall through the cracks if the wrong thing happens when they're insufficiently insured).

That said, we all have different conceptions of security (feeling safe and taken care of, whatever happens) and stability (feeling like we've properly balanced and reinforced important aspects of our lives), and these two sensibilities correlate with and are influenced by all sorts of factors.

Who we hang out with, for instance, can inform our sense of success, and that can distort our conception of what it means to be on stable economic ground.

We might also have friends who are ultra-assiduous about their health, maintaining sophisticated, time-consuming, and possibly expensive regimens to remain in solid shape (athletically, aesthetically, and maybe immunologically).

Such comparisons can make us feel like our own preparations are insufficient or unsound, when in reality they might be fine for us and our priorities, those other lifestyles and intended outcomes not worth the cost.

This can make us feel like we're missing something, not doing well enough, or that we're on shaky soil: our footing not as sure as we thought, our sense of balance and personal welfare diminished when measured according to someone else's metrics.

Understanding our own tolerance for risk and reinforcing ourselves accordingly is a ponderous task, with untold costs and payouts (most of which we hope to never need), and there's nothing wrong with trying out different stances to determine which suits of metaphorical armor are worth the price, and which would be (for us) a waste of (chronological, energetic, or monetary) capital.

Ensuring such coverage is available for a version of ourselves who is less fortunate, who's older and experiencing fresh age-related trials, or who simply has different needs and wants and priorities than we currently do can be worth the cost of entry, though, even if we have to stretch our imaginations and prognostications to justify paying for it.

Blank Spaces

In many books there are blank pages that were left so intentionally, sometimes to balance the number of pages in the folio (a packet of folded pages, stitched or glued to other packets along the book's spine), sometimes to manage the reader's experience (ensuring new chapters arrive on an odd-numbered "*recto*" page rather than an even-numbered "*verso*" page), and sometimes to leave room for notes the reader might want to jot while engaging with the printed work.

It's useful to leave intentional blank spaces in our lives, as well, as these unused tracts allow us to relax, decompress, assess, strategize, and unspool, calmly and ponderously parsing things that have happened and putting them into a useful context.

These spaces will sometimes be literal chunks of tangible real estate: uncluttered, unfilled portions of a room or the backyard meant to provide us with a meditative, unoccupied aesthetic when we would benefit from a change of scenery—an intentional extraction from our usual environments.

The spaces we occupy, especially familiar spaces, help shape our thinking because we encode memories in our rooms and shelves and the things we place on those shelves.

Our brains remember things in part based on relevant geographic data, and part of why "mind palaces" and similar memorization tricks work so well is that by mentally placing data in what feels like a physical location, or associating that data with things in our environments, we can more reliably and accurately summon it at will (brains are weird).

The same is true of tangible (non-imagined), familiar environments: we tuck information into these spaces, recalling something we need to do later in the evening when we glimpse a particular book, or thinking about the delicious anniversary dinner we had a few years ago any time we see the salt shaker on the kitchen table. We may even forget what we were thinking about if we cross the threshold into a different room, a tendency called "the doorway effect" that's predicated on the same general concept of storing information in our environments, as we then lose access to that stored information when we enter a new space.

Because we use familiar terrain in this way, going places (bodily, or in our minds) where the geospatial variables influencing our thinking are different can be useful if we want to consider things from another angle or break free from our typical cognitive rhythms.

We can also carve out psychological blank spaces: room on the calendar left intentionally unfilled so we can do whatever we feel like doing in the moment, including nothing at all (which can be more difficult than it sounds, as internal and social pressures encourage us to fill space).

That said, unclaimed spans of times are more attainable when we're also afforded some semblance of solitude, if only for a little while.

It's difficult, however, being alone if you're accustomed to (or crave) the opposite.

Despite that struggle, this muscle is worth training, as the longer we live, the more alone time we must endure, and such experiences can be agonizing or fulfilling, depending on how capable and confident we feel stepping into them.

People we love will leave us. They'll move away and they'll die. We'll go through breakups, we'll change jobs, and we'll move between schools, social groups, and familial arrangements.

Most of us will have plenty of opportunity to be alone over the course of our lives, so deciding to get better at embracing solitude—deciding to be alone but not lonely—is an investment worth making.

Loneliness needn't be a bad thing, either, as it can serve as a motivating force to get up in the morning, walk out the door, and go engage with our fellow humans (or other sorts of non-human life).

But embracing this concept, becoming more comfortable in our own exclusive company, being capable of keeping ourselves engaged and entertained and motivated and excited about life converts a frictionful, even frightening type of blank space into a conscious, confident, intentional act and exertion.

Bucket Lists

Bucket lists—the register of things we want to do before we "kick the bucket"—can be useful, but they can also lead us astray if we're not careful.

Many of us produce such lists during moments of enthusiasm and periods in which we feel a sense of expanded possibility (after holidays and birthdays, for instance). These are points at which we're rethinking everything, and it's a good idea to be brazen and dream big at such moments, as giving ourselves permission to deviate from our expected (and planned-for) path also provides us with the opportunity to question the nature and purpose of that path, and the steps we plan to take as we traverse it.

One of the potential downsides of having such a list, though, is that it's tempting to load it up with aspirational but conventional to-dos, which can commit our time, attention, and resources to goals we don't actually care about.

This is especially but not exclusively true of lists we make public.

When we display our ambitions for the world to see, we're incentivized to prioritize things that portray us in a positive light, based on the metrics we (and the social groups with which we want to align ourselves) care about.

So there's a lot of mountain-climbing and skydiving on these lists, even for those of us who don't particularly care about the outdoors or enjoy adrenaline-pumping activities. There's also a lot of book-writing, art-making, and other ambitious goals that seem externally impressive, but which don't actually line up with our broader collection of objectives and priorities.

It's possible we want to be seen as creative by our peers and this is one way to hint at our artistic ambitions (even if those ambitions don't line up with our heretofore lived reality), but we arguably have no reason (beyond posturing) to prioritize such goals over those that are actually meaningful to us, and which are thus aligned with our grander desires.

Bucket lists have a tendency to nudge us toward performative goal-setting, rather than a more practical and beneficial version of the same, and while it's wonderful to pursue aspirations that don't line up with how we've done things in the past (that's part of how we grow as people), it's also prudent to distinguish dissonant but truly desired outcomes from those that simply sound cool and which we hope will provide us with a veneer of intrigue or credibility.

Because of this tendency, and because we change so much over the course of our lives (including our long-term ambitions), it can sometimes be more productive to figure out what we don't care about and list those items (a reverse bucket list?), as that can free us up to pursue the unlisted stuff even more enthusiastically, and with greater focus.

As we grow older, one of the superpowers we develop is a slow-budding capacity to not care as much about what other people think. Not in the sense that we dismiss other people and their needs, and not in the sense that we become antisocially self-centered, but in the sense that external factors like cultural trends and other peoples' (and other entities') ideas have to compete with an increasingly refined assemblage of our own.

The older we get, the more this sense of self holds steady like a stone in a river as a deluge of influences flood past us, all hoping to knock us loose and tug us toward their priorities and perspectives.

We can strengthen this part of ourselves at any age, and doing so starts with becoming more aware of and honest about the things we do and don't want, do or don't like, and with allowing ourselves to question those tenets as we grow so they don't concretize into unassailable and ill-fitting dogma. We should be able to lean into these preferences, custom-tailoring our lives while still leaving room for who we want to become (and who we eventually do become) in the future.

The lists we make, bucket or reverse bucket, are part of that process.

They're loose, idealized plans that can orient us and our lives in various ways, and ideally that means helping to calibrate our compasses so they better reflect what we find vital and desirable, rather than pushing us toward generic, socially acceptable ambitions.

So we make lists, dream big, and get really expansive and excited about potential directions, goals, and the steps we might take to achieve them. But we hopefully do so in a way that reflects who we are now and who we'd like to become, rather than reaching into other people's buckets and unquestioningly plopping whatever we find there into our own.

Generations

The concept of generational delineations, which are more formally called "age cohorts," has helped shape our collective perception of age since the mid-19th century.

Because people who are born, grow into toddlers, go through teenagerdom, graduate, become parents, and retire during a given span of time in a particular region are influenced by similar variables (politics, economics, social mores, and so on), this theory says there are generalizations we can make about them.

Such generalizations can be useful for predicting the wants and needs of these groups, how they'll behave in various contexts, how they'll vote and what they'll buy, and how they might respond to change.

That's the demographic definition of the term, at least.

In other fields of study, "generation" refers to the parent-child dynamic, one generation begetting the next, that younger generation eventually siring and raising another, still-younger generation, on and on and on, this lineage traceable as far back into history as written documents and oral tradition illuminate.

Both conceptions of generation can be useful in that they help us understand, for instance, which age grouping of people lived through a particular historical event (like WWII) and how that experience may have shaped their beliefs and behaviors, which in turn can shape the beliefs and behaviors of their offspring.

The same can be true, according to this conception, of technological developments like the smartphone, and shifts in norms like how people dress and which ideologies hold the most sway in governance—so it's not just scarring (and geopolitics-rearranging) military conflicts, it's everything.

By looking at these influences (and secondary influences, like being raised by someone who lived through WWII) we can come to know things about, for instance, 20-somethings who came of age in the mid-2020s, and that can help us figure out the right messaging (and medium for said messaging) if we want to convince this group to not smoke tobacco products, to vote for a particular candidate, or to buy a specific brand of soap.

This sort of data is collected, aggregated, bought and sold, and wielded by entities ranging from governments to snack food conglomerates.

The accuracy of generational assumptions is questionable, as any sweeping statements we make about US-based Gen Xers or Baby Boomers may be statistically sound, but not applicable to any individual whose age places them in those categories.

Regardless, generational theory has had a substantial influence on cultural, economic, and political thought, and it has shaped our assumptions about such groups as a result.

It's important to note that although many big, powerful entities take this sort of data seriously (because it can sometimes divine non-obvious information about groups of people), generational designations are not destiny. This is true of claims about what such groups are supposedly thinking, wanting, and where they're headed, and it's even more true of individual people we slot into these cohorts, the labels we slap on them often wrong in every specific.

Despite their flaws, we continue to treat these data points and models as if they're infallible, partly because so many entities have invested so much in them, and partly because they do sometimes get things right at the macro level, and that can be useful in the same way it's useful to predict where vast herds of elk will migrate next.

The trouble is that we often treat this data as if it can accurately predict where a single elk will wander, which couldn't be further from the truth.

Since we started categorizing society in this way, the youngest groups, those at the bottom of every temporal heap, have been near-universally derided, their elders confounded by and concerned about their norms, preferences, and ambitions, and the youths consequently viewed as potential but failing solutions to all the world's problems.

Members of more aged generations almost always forget that their elders leveled the same accusations at them when they were inelegant and naïve (relative) toddlers, and this generational amnesia is part of why the tradition of looking down upon the youngest contemporary contingent persists.

Repeated often enough—by our elders, by analysts, and by pop cultural narratives—we may come to believe these confident-sounding but oft-inaccurate claims, incorporating them into our sense of who we are, how we should think, and what we should prioritize.

I've been through this wringer as an older Millennial, and I was told from early on that my generation is ruining the economy, that we're unable to function in the real world, and that we're perpetual children, clinging to our parents and the trappings of youth due to some kind of ingrained Peter Pan complex.

Some of these claims are probably real in the sense that a statistically high number of Millennials lived with their parents into their 20s and 30s (longer than preceding generations). But the rationale for that trend (a refusal to "grow up," according to the standards of adulthood held by previous generations) is arguably incorrect: we Millennials entered the workforce at a truly brutal moment (an economic collapse) and then suffered through a series of other catastrophes (including a global pandemic) during our prime money-earning years.

Given that, a sluggish transition into the real estate-owning (or even apartment-renting) stage of our lives is perhaps to be expected.

Similarly, the advent of widespread personal computer (and then smartphone) ownership probably influenced the views and behaviors of Millennials more than other generations because we were young enough to experience that shift in our formative years, but were still old enough to understand, remember, and earnestly embrace it.

Technological, communication, and work- and entertainment-related paradigm-shifts hit everyone hard, so limiting our search for related (and perhaps causal) changes to the youngest generation is not a fair or complete analysis. But we can sometimes note these shifts and make guesses about how they may influence the collective nature of a cohort, and periodically those guesses will be somewhat accurate (at the herd scale, not at the level of an individual).

Conjectures related to the youngest demographics with the most life (and the largest number of possibilities) ahead of them are ostensibly the most valuable, which could explain why attempting to predict our youngest cohorts' next steps seems to be such a popular pastime in so many societies.

When we discuss generations culturally, though, these labels can become something like sports teams or political parties, all of us building up and celebrating our own groups while criticizing and scapegoating the others.

Society often blames those with relatively less power for its ills, while those with more power, who have more opportunity to shape the narrative because of their positions, prestige, and resources, will be portrayed in a more favorable light.

Just as our geographies of origin, our faiths or the schools we attend, the work we do or the parents we have can significantly influence who we become, how we live, and what we care about, then, generational designations—or our biases of them, at least—can reshape our perceptions of ourselves and others, even if they're not destiny, and even if they often fail to say anything of fundamental importance (or with any veracity) about us, individually.

Crises

The popular media trope of the middle-aged man, flush with money and freshly divorced, awkwardly (for everyone) going through the motions of a youth he's attempting to reclaim, isn't the only version of the midlife crisis portrayed in popular media, but it's the most common.

Whatever the specifics, such portrayals feature characters who are trying to figure out who they are after they've hit something approximating the mid-point of their statistical lifespans.

From birth to death, we may go through many crises of this kind. Our brains rebel against changes we can feel in our physicalities and thinking, unwilling to accept a new reality that's beginning to shape everything we do and experience.

These moments seem to appear out of nowhere, first when we hit puberty, then after the responsibilities of early adulthood have set in, and once more when we reach our 40s or 50s and realize we haven't accomplished everything we'd hoped to accomplish.

As we tumble into the second-half of our lives, we may struggle to figure out who we will be from that point forward, lacking the definitional aid of our careers, family-rearing responsibilities, and sometimes without our long leaned-upon romantic partners, either.

Whenever they arrive, whatever their triggers, these moments of jarring realization, of stunned "is this it?" questioning, of deep-felt mortality, fresh aches, and new (perhaps less favorable) social categorizations, can be difficult.

Some people are utterly roiled in these moments, experiencing significant adjustments to their overall valence, tilting from optimism into pessimism or even despondency when the reality of their situation hits home. They eventually start walking the path toward some kind of acceptance, but that journey, too, can be stressful, tumultuous, and painful.

There's no one age at which we're most crisis-prone, in part because we're all different people, physically and mentally, and in part because there are different external forces acting upon us, our lives, and our self-perceptions.

We enter the workforce at different ages, having lived through different childhood and educational experiences. We retire (or realize we're unable to) at different times, and we wake up and realize we're perceptually "old" in the eyes of other people at diverse moments.

These periods are informed by a slew of compounding and interacting variables, ranging from the relationships we're in, how healthy or unhealthy we are (and how healthy or unhealthy we feel), the work we do, the psychological wellbeing we enjoy or lack, and where our portfolio of assets (money, job title, looks, charisma) positions us on the spectrum of mainstream attractiveness.

These age-related crises, then, are varied enough that it's impossible to say anything about them that will apply to every single person's experience.

That said, the question of who we are separate from our work, accomplishments, and other status symbols sparks some such crises.

Who am I beyond my job, the title it grants me, the resources I earn by performing it, and the time and effort I invest in it? Who am I separate from my non-work responsibilities, the roles I play in other people's lives, and the impact I have on fields and in spaces I care about?

We may feel unrepresented by the things we do, the titles we wear, and the impact we're able to have on the world—or we may feel like that's all we have.

The gap between our perception of self and our outward-facing expression of the same can both cause and amplify crises, as might worries that we've wasted gobs of time, significant portions of our finite lives, on stuff that doesn't actually matter (or matter to us).

Our conception of what's important, good, and moral changes over time, too, as we learn more about ourselves and the world.

Such changes can motivate us to overcompensate when we realize something is different, and we may, consequently, go through a year in which we quit our accountancy jobs to become dancers, divorce our long-term partners out of the blue, and buy sports cars, because why not?

There's nothing inherently wrong with any of these decisions, but sudden, jolting shifts of this kind can leave us feeling empty if we're not careful: simply doing the opposite of what we've always done will not necessarily fulfill us, and pursuing novelty for the sake of novelty can leave us in essentially the same position as before, but with fewer resources and strong relationships upon which we can rely.

Rather than engaging in mood-swing-like behavior, it may be more prudent to use these moments as fuel for intentional changes made over time.

We can learn to more skillfully navigate these crisis moments, too, if we allow ourselves to acknowledge that our midlife or other crises might look different from what we expect them to look like, and if we build scaffoldings that can help shield us from the worst impacts of such moments.

One useful scaffolding worth considering is a habit of checking in with ourselves, regularly, maybe through therapy sessions, maybe by taking up meditation or journaling.

These sorts of practices help us maintain a sense of who we are and what we're going through, and that can allow us to address pebble-sized problems before they can aggregate into a landslide.

Such habits can also help us make confident changes to our lives when warranted, because we will enjoy an up-to-date sense of who we are and what we care about, and that enables us to make more precise and accurate lifestyle alterations, when alterations are justified.

Energy

Most modern electrical grids work roughly the same way: our energy sources (power plants, solar farms, wind turbines) are plugged into a mesh of cables that funnel energy from place to place, substations strategically located across the network transform the transported energy to align with local needs, and a bunch of devices scattered across the grid track the electricity, amplify it so it can travel further, truncate it for final delivery, and provide insulation to reduce noise and prevent energy loss.

That insulation is important, as a fair bit of transmitted electricity is emitted as heat while it's being funneled from source to user: something like 2% on long-range, high-voltage lines, and around 4% on low-voltage lines (the kind that pipe energy from the high-voltage cables to our homes and other buildings).

There's also a lot of loss at the source, though, as even the most efficient production-scale solar panels are (at the moment) only about 23% efficient, and most power plants generate heat by burning something (like coal) or via nuclear or concentrated solar power, which converts water into steam, which spins a turbine. This process is only about 35% efficient, two-thirds of the generated energy wasted instead of being converted into electricity.

I find this to be a useful metaphor and mental model for my personal energy levels, because it lines up with (and underlines) some of the processes animating my brain and body.

I'm fueled by all sorts of things, including (in a literal sense) food and water, and (in a figurative sense) learning about unfamiliar subjects, deep conversations, and pursuing outcomes I care about.

There are drains on the total amount of energy produced via these and other sources, though, including not eating or drinking the right things ("right" in this context referring to the correct inputs for maximal energetic production), not spending time with the right people (or spending too much time with the wrong people), and investing too much of myself in things that deplete rather than fuel me.

Time-wasting habits, self-defeating heuristics and assumptions, and ways of thinking about the world that are incorrect or incomplete can become (often invisible) vampire drains on all that energy, akin to unnecessary or unused devices that are left plugged in all day, draining resources from the system but providing nothing of value of in return.

There's seepage and loss and waste, then, which means there's plenty of opportunity to make things more efficient and effective by coming up with overhauls and tweaks that inject more energy into the system or which preserve more of what's already there.

So if I realize that my habit of eating certain types of foods or eating at a specific time of day makes me tired in the afternoon, adjusting, halting, or replacing that habit can net me outsized results from a tiny change: all of my afternoons suddenly more enjoyable and useful, and all I have to do is eat at a different time, or stop eating sluggishness-inducing things.

Similarly, I might keep tabs on my relationships, my career, my workout routine, or my hobbies to see what's producing what, and what's hurting me more than helping, as over time this can illuminate paths by which I'll be able to add more energy into the mix and address preventable drains on the system.

This is an engineery, designerly way of looking at an often abstract concept, I know, and it won't resonate with everyone. But especially as I've gotten older, I've realized that small changes can lead to substantial positive outcomes if these changes apply to holistic systems that affect many aspects of our lives.

Thinking about such things in terms that show their interconnectedness and remind me of just how handleable some of these issues can be makes it more likely I notice and address them, rather than continuing to suffer their downsides because of ignorance or passivity.

Wisdom

We needn't be brilliant or informed to be wise: the accumulation of wisdom only requires we pay attention and learn from our experiences.

So while it certainly doesn't hurt to know more about more things and to aim for generalism (paired with intentional investments in deeper expertise) in our pursuit of knowledge and know-how, we can have little in the way of formal education or trained, monetizable comprehension and still possess wisdom about people, life, and other things we've had the chance to mull over.

"Wisdom" is a fluffy term that means different things to different people, but in general it means possessing sound judgement and a way of looking at things that brings clarity and leads to positive outcomes, rather than amplifying muddlement and error. To be wise is to have a perspective that's broad or incisive or unusually clear, and maybe all of these things.

Some people possess innate worldviews or heuristics that enable them to perceive things in this way, seemingly from birth, while others achieve the same through living, growing, experiencing, and reflecting on what they have seen, done, and learned.

In this way (for many of us, at least), wisdom arrives in drips, drabs, and doses as we progress through life, and what seems like the deepest, most meaningful and insightful thing in the world to me at age 15 might be obviously superficial or flat-out wrong by the time I'm 25.

Age by age, each new version of ourselves thinks and understands within the context of more life lived, more knowledge gained, more comprehension gleaned, and with a heightened capacity to compile all that new acumenical grist into actionable, sharable revelations.

Much of what we might eventually think of as wisdom arrives in atomic units: moments in time and segments of knowledge that, once internalized, can serve as (or be woven into) lessons.

We'll encounter some lessons over and over, needing several exposures before we soak them up, or even recognize them as valuable (or as lessons).

Often we encounter lessons when we're not in a receptive mind-state, which is a bit like being handed a beverage when we're not thirsty; it's right there, but we have no inclination to imbibe it.

We may also encounter lessons that will someday open up to us, but which, upon first contact, we lack the experience (or other prerequisites) to notice, assess, and appreciate them. Thus, our acquisition of these potential seeds of wisdom is postponed until we grow into who we need to be to understand and appreciate them.

Some wisdom, like some knowledge, seems to push us toward a specific next step and a progression of understandings that often (though not inevitably) guide us from one revelation to the next.

Other bits of wisdom slam us into walls, requiring we reassess how we've been applying them (possibly for years), which can result in a difficult reckoning and an even more difficult transition toward some other (previously unseen, ignored, or dismissed) path.

Wisdom isn't provable or testable in the way you might show a mathematical equation is true or that a scientific finding is almost certainly accurate. Wisdom is a way of looking at things that illuminates an aspect of life or perspective that was previously concealed from us, and it's a means of weaving disparate elements into a more cohesive, comprehensible, manageable whole.

It's important to note that not all lessons are beneficial.

Who among us didn't learn, at some point in our lives, to not try too hard because doing so can lead to failure, pain, and embarrassment?

This isn't a productive lesson, but we may cling to it as dogma as our brains attempt to protect us from the psychological slings and arrows of life, guiding us toward paths that seem safer and more secure (from the standpoint of never facing risk), but which might also be numbing, negative, and limiting.

We have to be careful, then, which lessons we decide to incorporate into our mental rulebooks and life-shaping heuristics.

Ideally, in addition to developing filters for undeserving bits of (apparent) wisdom, we also periodically cull old stuff that's been proven wrong or that no longer serves us. Wisdom isn't static, it's an ever-developing sense of the world that helps us make better judgments over time, and our sense of what's sensible will change as we change.

It's also important to remember that we all learn at unique moments and cadences.

While there are things we'll be more likely to learn at certain ages because of the variables to which an average person of a particular age in a given culture is exposed, assuming that someone who's 40 will know what it means to be a parent or that someone who's 50 will understand how to be in a healthy romantic relationship is not prudent or fair.

We achieve these milestones at different times, if we achieve them at all (which isn't a given), and that's the nature of things no matter how desperately we might want to simplify and stratify, formalizing the acquisition of wisdom into something akin to learning our multiplication tables or how to punctuate a paragraph.

Wisdom is both a pursuit and a skill we can exercise, and that means living more (and a more diversified) life can help us see more clearly and make better decisions as we grow older, but also that thinking about how we perceive, how we decide, what metrics we use for this process, and how we might improve upon that jumble of interconnected steps and systems can help us become more sagacious and sharp as we accrue more years, knowledge, and practical prowess.

Meaning

Logotherapy is a field that's entirely focused on meaning and how it motivates us in various ways.

Whether or not you buy into concepts like psychotherapy and existential analysis (from which logotherapy takes inspiration), it's worth considering how meaning fuels and drains us, and how this notion develops and changes as we grow older.

Psychiatrists who use logotherapeutic frameworks contend that life has meaning, even in the most horrible, seemingly pointless moments, and that pursuing meaning (in all its permutations) is what gives our day-to-day existence purpose.

The idea, then, is that in trying to discover what it's all for, why we're here, what's the point, we go through the motions of living, experiencing and surviving even horrible situations because this pursuit unto itself can be valuable, fulfilling, and satisfying enough to keep us going.

In this way, seeking significance is purposeful because doing so helps us believe there's something at the end of the path we're walking, and that allows us to persist even when it seems like we have no reason to.

We can see a more grounded (and less philosophical) version of this concept in how we approach goals.

We all have goals, whether they're front of mind or subconsciously informing our actions throughout the day, and the achievement of these goals (or portions of them, or side-quests associated with them) feels good.

Being capable of setting ambitious but still attainable goals is therefore a skill worth honing, as it helps us carve the paths we'll walk throughout our lives and offers us things to desire, alongside opportunities to experience the satisfaction of accomplishment.

Some of us, because we've been incredibly successful (in our work, relationships, or the acquisition of knowledge), or because we've been unambitious with our goal-setting (only pursuing immediately attainable outcomes), will at some point have achieved everything we ever wanted to achieve.

Maybe we desired gobs of money and a great big house, and we wake up one day and realize, wow, we did it. The house is gorgeous and huge, and we have more money than we could ever reasonably spend.

Or maybe we wanted to be the most well-regarded lawyer in our legal niche, to build the biggest of a specific type of tech startup, or we wanted to have a loving partner and seven kids, and huh—we did it. We're living the dream.

Sometimes, though, crossing that finish line will not feel how we expected it to feel. We'll have everything we ever wanted and yet feel lost, rudderless, incomplete. This can be a tough moment, especially if the idea of the journey being the destination is a foreign concept.

That it might be healthy to set more and ever-more impressive goals as we grow can seem counterintuitive, as most of the games we play and ambitions we pursue have well-defined beginnings and endings: finishing them is the point of starting them, and committing to more and more difficult pursuits keeps us from winning.

A key tenet of logotherapy and many other meaning-related fields, though, is that it's important to be capable not just of crossing finish lines, but also identifying and building entirely new race tracks so that we have more things to pursue when we finish a heretofore life-defining challenge.

This is especially vital if we're competitive and have dedicated ourselves to achieving substantial goals, but it's also important if we've set goals that are moderate and attainable. In both cases, we're likely to reach the end of our to-do lists at some point and will need something new in which to invest ourselves, lest we someday suffer a sudden absence of aspiration and find ourselves with no idea how to spend our time and energy.

Accomplishment can be both boon and burden. We can scrape and scramble and work ourselves to the bone to realize an outcome that seems meaningful from a distance, only to discover, once manifested, that it's not. It wasn't actually the goal that drove us: attempting to accomplish it was the source of our motive power and gratification all along.

While it's valuable to develop our capacity for goal-setting, it's also worth understanding the concept of the Hedonic Treadmill, which says that although we might experience increases or decreases in happiness over time, our sense of satisfaction and fulfillment will reset to a default "not great, not horrible" setting no matter how high or low it periodically flutters.

A slower burning life rich with interesting pursuits and a sense of meaning, then, may lead to better outcomes, as wringing ourselves out for what we assume will be huge and permanent improvements to our sense of happiness and actualization will instead (if we're lucky) grant us a few brief moments of what we hoped for before we revert to that neutral state. This misalignment of expectation and outcome can spark a cycle of burnout and an unhealthy (and unrealistic) pursuit of happiness that negatively shapes our lives, if we're not careful.

Maintaining a steady pace along a path filled with interesting challenges, though, all of them just beyond what we're capable of today, provides an appealing balance of growth-inducing effort, regular and fulfilling victories, and a sustainable rhythm that allows us to appreciate and benefit from the journey.

Self-Truthfulness

I don't know what I'm doing.

One of the most wonderful surprises as I've gotten older has been the ease with which I can say this, can mean it, and can do so without suffering any ego bruises or pernicious self-judgement.

I allow myself to not know. I acknowledge my ignorance and incapacity, and I make these shortfalls public when doing so will help me remedy them, or when it will serve other purposes, like differentiating an uninformed opinion from an informed one. And despite these acknowledgements and disclosures (and in some ways, because of them) I still feel happy, confident, and capable.

None of which means I'm 100% comfortable in my own skin, nor that I feel sure of myself, what I (think I) know, or the decisions I make; if anything, I'm less certain today than I've been at any other moment in my life.

But that lack of certainty, that dearth of baseless self-surety, counterintuitively makes it more likely I'll end up where I want to be, soaking up inputs that are more aligned with reality and walking a path that makes sense for who I am and where I'd actually like to go, rather than down some random thoroughfare offered by fate and chosen by my unwavering (but hollow) sense of conviction.

It's important, I think, to be truthful with ourselves about everything.

No amount of investment or optimization will get us where we need to be if we're aiming for the wrong outcomes, and we're more likely to calibrate our compasses to the wrong magnetic north if we don't have a sincere and sharp sense of who we are, what we want, and why we want what we want.

Taking the time to know and understand ourselves, and to develop habits that ensure we continue to do so as we grow and change is important, then, as we're more prone to pursuing someone else's idea of an ideal life lacking this knowledge and these systems.

This isn't as easy as it sounds, unfortunately, as countless external and internal variables distort the raw information we soak up, shaping our perceptions about the world, about other people, and about ourselves, like curved lenses over our eyes.

Thus, even achieving self-awareness, much less self-truthfulness, can be quite the task, requiring we become increasingly conscious of our own biases and prejudices, our own blindspots and out-of-proportion emphases, and that we do our best to correct for them, just as we might wear glasses or contact lenses to adjust blurry eyesight.

Figuring out the right prescription can be a tedious task, though, as it's not just one lens we have to account for, but a boundless number of them, all stacked atop each other, their deformations aggregating into a kind of ultra-prescription that malforms and misrepresents reality in complex ways.

It's possible to become more aware of and account for these variables, but we can only ever make an imperfect attempt because of the depth and ever-shifting nature of the issue.

With this in mind, it's prudent we maintain a sense of humility.

Something I've had to remind myself of semi-regularly over the years is that I'm happiest, most fulfilled, and I do my best work when I'm the most refined version of myself that I can muster.

I've needed those reminders because there are so many forces in the world nudging us to be someone else, or some other version of ourselves that better resonates with the incentives and wants and priorities of other people and entities.

We know what lifestyle choices, business models, approaches to health, daily routines, faith, morality, and everything else work for other people: we're blunderbussed with that information daily. Look at these people! Look how great and cool and impressive their lives are!

The implicit message is "be like them and you'll also be financially successful and beautiful and your life will be the envy of everyone you know," but that's not true, as there's plenty of luck and happenstance and serendipity woven into every single human being's story. So the same actions performed by different people will not typically result in the same outcomes.

It's not always pleasant reminding ourselves that being more "us" is ideal, because that means there's no model, no guidebook, no set of instructions that can tell us, step-by-step, how to accomplish our dreams (or even more fundamentally: what our dreams should be).

We have to invent all of this stuff from nothing, cobbling together an us-shaped set of beliefs and ambitions, alongside the means to align ourselves with and pursue them, and that's just bogglingly difficult; it's the labor of a lifetime.

I've also had to remind myself, in recent years, that sometimes I'll feel confident in my handling of all this responsibility—being more me and charting a custom path for myself—and in others I will feel like an absolute failure.

Sometimes I feel like I've got it all together, know exactly where I am, who I am, where I'm going, and how to get there, but the next day I might stumble into a new, multi-day or multi-year period of tumult and uncertainty, stumbling my way toward another relatively stable situation where I'll be able to feel (temporarily) confident again.

In between, though, I will feel lost.

I'll be scrambling for meaning, reminders of self-worth, and anything I can scavenge that helps me feel secure, worthy, and okay.

Those in-between moments aren't easy, but I've been through enough of them that I'm usually able to recognize them for what they are (though sometimes it takes a little while to realize that's what's happening, even now).

These fresh paths do eventually lead me to something better than what I left behind. I just have to fumble through the wildness a bit before I get there, and before I even have a sense of what "there" might be.

Learning

Over the past decade, I've cultivated the habit of looking things up when I realize I don't understand them as fully as I previously assumed.

This might happen mid-conversation or while I'm writing about something that bumps up against another, less-well-understood topic. In any such case, when I notice I don't grok something as well as I thought I did (or at all), I whip out my phone (or open a browser window on my computer) and start googling, Wikipedia-ing, and clicking on links.

In the modern, interconnected world, a thorough explanation for pretty much everything is just a click or two away, and I can usually fill even wide knowledge-gaps within a few minutes—though I'm careful to make a note (in a digital document maintained for this purpose) of any concepts I'd like to explore more deeply later, and I keep tabs on which resources are reliable for which sorts of information so I can filter out deceptive and nonsensical content.

The point of this habit is to expose myself to concepts and understandings I wouldn't otherwise have had a reason to think about or pursue. Developing exploration-related reflexes can make learning-for-depth a casual, lifelong pursuit, rather than a task relegated to school or work; moments in which we're forced to learn something in order to pass a test or get paid, and thus not the best contexts for sparking new passions or enjoying moments of awe.

I experimented for a while, years ago, with becoming a coffee connoisseur. It seemed like something I might like, and the products used to make coffee at a high level tend to be nicely designed, so there was an aesthetic benefit to this undertaking, as well.

After a lot of reading, experimenting, and coffee tastings ("cuppings"), though, I realized I would probably benefit most from medium-grade coffee beans, processed using inexpensive hardware, with relatively low-key (but not passive) effort, rather than anything more sophisticated, expensive, or high-end.

Figuring out what we enjoy, what fuels us, what stokes curiosity and awe, and what tests our limits is fundamental to habitual learning. But it's also important to be capable of exploring, experimenting, wholeheartedly engaging, and then shelving such pursuits when appropriate.

We only have so much time, energy, and resources to spend because life is finite, as is the number of hours (or minutes) we have available to invest in educational activities each day.

It's vital that we allow ourselves to set aside or re-relegate something to a back-burner (or other location of lesser focus and investment) if we want to accumulate an abundance of varied knowledge, rather than limiting ourselves to an understanding of one or two facets of the world.

It's useful to think of learning as a seasonal thing in which there are periods of intense exploration, moments in which we exploit that which we've previously learned and experienced, and pockets of time in which we're optimized and primed for resting, mulling, considering, analyzing, stepping back, and sharing what we've picked up with others.

Cycling between such seasons allows us to maintain our curiosity and investigatory instincts, while also carving out space for internal processing of what we've learned, and for amalgamating all that knowledge and know-how into different shapes for personal and societal benefit.

A conception of learning in which there's a period during our youth in which we learn, and then a second period in which we coast on those lessons for the rest of our lives, in contrast, puts us on a path toward stagnation and developmental quiescence.

Such an approach also fails to prepare us for a rapidly changing world in which the half-life of knowledge (the time it takes for half of what we know to no longer be true, relevant, or applicable because of new discoveries and developments, and the advent of new tools and norms) is shrinking.

This division of life into two segments, "education" and "everything else," no longer works, if it ever did, and it's not great for our economies and cultures but it also leaves us in the lurch, individually, as we grow increasing disconnected from the ever-iterating world—the gap between us and the rest of humanity expanding at the pace of progress.

It's important that we have a sense of how much of what we think we know is actually true (and something we know, rather than something we can quickly search for online, if we need to) so we can fill limiting blank-spots in our grasp of the world, and reinforce the foundations of our understandings.

It's important that we figure out sustainable habits and postures toward learning that allow us to weave this sort of growth into our lives for the long-term, rather than hoping that periodic brushes with knowledge will give us what we need to remain a relevant civilizational component.

And it's important that we can manage and deploy our learning-related resources, lest we find ourselves overspecialized, unbalanced, and incapable of reorienting as the world changes around us, and as we change from within: both transformations demanding a detour that we want to ensure we can make.

Informational Inputs

After hearing a new song, we're no longer the same people we were before we heard it.

The change might be so insignificant that it can barely be said to have happened: our brains storing a hint of a suggestion of a reference to the beat, lyrics, rhythm, and the unique combination of aural elements, all ensuring that if we hear the song again, it'll feel familiar.

Sometimes the change is more substantial, though.

Sometimes we hear the right song at the right moment, and that motivates us to do something we might not otherwise have done (or done the way we did it, or done as well as we did it).

Sometimes we listen to a sad song and it brings us (and our whole day) down. Sometimes we listen to an upbeat song and it helps us hit a new exercise milestone, which then influences all of our future workouts.

This relationship we have with information is part of what informs my approach to informational inputs: I don't want to suffer from an overwhelming deluge of stimuli, but I also don't want to wobble through the world lacking the understanding necessary to pursue my priorities and to serve as a valuable member of my communities.

There's a balance point, then, at which I'm able to get what I need and want from data, qualia, knowledge, gossip, entertainment, and all the other sources of me-changing words, atoms, bytes, and music notes, but at which there are no superfluous inputs; I get what I need and want, but only that.

This is an issue of consumption, and as with other types of consumption we're prone to overindulgence on one hand, and dangerous levels of self-denial on the other; though neither extreme serves us as well as an intentionally plotted middle ground.

Both ends of that spectrum are easier to maintain than the middle, however, because no rebalancing is required on the fringes: you can basically just hurl yourself bodily in either direction, rather than having to make conscious (and semi-regular) decisions about inputs, taking responsibility for their measurement and maintenance.

I think about this balancing act as curating my inputs, because just like curating a library of books or a gallery full of artwork, it requires intent and care, and it demands we consider the big picture rather than fixating on individual elements in isolation.

I want to be healthy, fulfilled, excited about life, to feel generally good, to know about things, and to be exposed to new potential passions while also feeling free to cultivate those that've already caught my interest.

In addition to wanting to curate a personal portfolio of inputs that are valuable (and often enjoyable) unto themselves, then, I want to make sure the overall informational flow helps me grow and learn and feel good in its totality, and that it provides me with the information I need to enjoy more freedom and capacity in the future, while also helping me remain psychologically healthy, civically engaged, and so on.

One of the most fundamental elements of a well-considered, healthy info-diet is the perceptual distance between us and what we're consuming.

World news delivers data about things happening on the other side of the planet, sometimes even off-planet. Local news contains similar information about what's happening in my country, city, or neighborhood, but typically focuses on people I don't personally know, or even know of.

Information about my friends and family—their struggles and stresses, victories and accomplishments—is also news, though of a far more personal flavor. Things happening in my life, my household, my own in-person relationships even more directly influence the shape of my day-to-day life.

And my internal ebbs and flows, efforts and goals, curiosities and experiments are the most local news of all, originating within my brain and body, and informing how I think, what I do, and the choices I make.

All of these informational orbits are important, and all of them could affect my life and the people and things I care about.

A disaster in China might not seem immediately relevant to me, but that disaster could spark supply chain ripples that eventually increase the cost of a smartphone I was planning to buy, which could mean I have to work more hours before I can afford it, all that extra work disrupting my life in numerous concrete ways.

An obscure change in city policy may not seem important to understand, at first, but that change could eventually lead to a shift in traffic patterns, economic hardships for friends, or the closure of a beloved neighborhood bookstore. Lacking such policy knowledge, the votes we cast may not line up with our priorities and beliefs.

Wherever it originates, then, information from across chronological, cultural, regional, and proximate strata can shape the course of my life, even if the path from Point A to Point B isn't always obvious, at first.

Information also arrives at different speeds and cadences.

A book is less likely to imbue up-to-the-millisecond information, but it may deliver narrative and understanding with greater depth and substance than what's contained in the average social post or short form video.

Likewise, while quick sips of gossip consumed with our morning coffee and enjoyed with a friend from work can be valuable, so too can longer, more meandering and philosophically robust conversational explorations with strangers we meet at train stations and after church services.

All sources are thus potentially worthy of our time and attention, however fast they move and however distant (and intuitively irrelevant to us) their origin may seem.

Incorporating at least a little of each type—some neighborhood-level gossip, some world news, some national intrigue, some internal revelations—seems to bear the best fruit, though it sometimes may be prudent to focus on just one or a few informational orbits, depending on where we're at in life and what we're up to.

Whatever our momentary focus, it's also important to consider the sources of the information we take in.

The news in particular can be stressful, anxiety-inducing, in-group-reinforcing, and littered with misleading, misinformed, and heavily biased takes.

There are things we can do to make our news-consumption habits more productive, including avoiding most TV news, avoiding editorial and opinion content, and sticking with journalistic entities with the right economic incentives and reputations for non-polemical coverage. If we only hear takes that agree with our existing worldviews and political biases, we're not watching or reading or listening to the news, we're enjoying politics-themed entertainment and propaganda.

Social networks can be used critically and productively, but many of these platforms are actively harmful to discourse, to critical thinking skills, and to their users' capacity to focus on, engage with, and consider things beyond the superficial and ideologically slanted.

There's potential value there, then, just as there's potential value in purely entertainment-oriented reality television, but we really have to think carefully about how we consume such things, in what doses, and in combination with which other informational elements to ensure we're not flattening our perceptions of the world and of other people, as a consequence.

One trick I find to be useful when I'm feeling overwhelmed by serious, real-deal news and similar inputs is stepping back to establish a less hardcore, more sustainable and loose data-imbibing routine for a time.

I think of this as maintaining a global situational awareness—a general sense of what's going on in the world —which allows me to remain of the world without feeling the need to become a scholar in every conflict, development, or political narrative.

This lower-impact baseline is a lot easier to sustain in terms of time and energy, but it still gives us what we need to update our mental maps of what's going on and how everything fits together so we can easily plug back into the larger, denser jumble of available information when we're ready to do so.

Finally, it's worth remembering that every single thing we learn, experience, and are told is filtered through us-specific perceptual lenses that are shaped by our current understandings and assumptions about the world, ourselves, and other people.

We can't remove these lenses (they're part of the human experience), but we can account for them, working this knowledge into our learning process and doing our best to correct for the perceptual distortion they apply to everything we soak up.

Perception of Age

As I write this, I'm just a few months from my 39th birthday, but my internal perception of my age is somewhere in my late-20s.

It's possible this miscalibration is the consequence of something me-specific in how I think, but there's evidence that many of us perceive ourselves to be different ages than we actually are and that these perceptions may both reflect and be reflected by our bodily and cognitive experiences.

Researchers coined the term "subjective age" to refer to an intuitively experienced age that differs from our true, biological version of the same.

Studies looking into this topic have shown that while we don't actually believe we're different ages than we are, there's often a contrast between our knee-jerk, "I feel like I'm this many years old" reflex, and the number of years we've accumulated.

Some researchers believe that this distinction is partly due to external factors, such as how others treat us, the types of work and activities we participate in, the nature of our relationships, and how we feel, cognitively and in terms of overall health.

Someone who's fit, doesn't have chronic pain, and who goes out dancing regularly with their friends may just latently feel younger than someone the same age who suffers from lower-back issues and who spends all their time working in an office, paying bills, and taking care of their children, because we associate these things with different periods of life, those associations shaped by cultural mores and by media depictions of varying age groups.

Some research has shown than an internal sense of youth can motivate us to do more youth-associated things, which can reinforce our feeling of youthfulness because we feel good, we go do the things we like to do when we feel good, and that creates a feedback loop that amplifies our sense of being younger.

The same may be true in the other direction, as well. Degraded health, adulthood-tinged responsibilities, and a sense of sameness or roteness can feel like "oldness" because of our cultural associations with these things, and because it may contrast with how we felt and how we spent our time earlier in life. An internal feeling of "getting old" can nudge us to do more old-valenced things, these behaviors can then reinforce oldness-associated factors (like a bad back and routine lifestyle), and the cycle may then self-perpetuate, our feeling of frailty becoming stronger and more present.

This will vary from person to person, and though most adults who have taken part in this type of research perceive themselves to be an average of about 20% younger than they are, there's a huge range of potentiality here, including some people who age themselves up, though that appears to be rarer than aging ourselves perpetually downward.

This is interesting in part because of what it suggests about the concept of age (much of it is in our heads), but also because of what it says about our internalized beliefs about people of different ages.

The whole idea of being a late-bloomer implies that there is a proper, normal age at which to do various things, when in reality we all mature at different rates for different aspects of our lives. For some of us, the socially acceptable version of "maturity" will never arrive because that specific conception of what it means to be mature doesn't resonate with (or make sense to) us.

Those shared narratives about age, and our consequent expectations of people who have accumulated more years than we have, I suspect, contribute to assumptions held by many that our own twilight eras will be washed-out photocopies of our earlier years, rather than novel progressions.

Modern medicine being flawed but miraculous compared to what even our grandparents enjoyed, our 40s have in some ways become a continuation of our earlier decades of life.

Said another way, our 40s are the entry point to a new adolescence, and we're both empowered and hampered by the assets and baggage we accumulate until that point, similar to what we go through in our early adulthood.

Thinking in these terms, and not just for our 40s, but also our 50s, 60s, 70s, and onward, leaves room for a lot more life. It gives us permission to orient toward growth and involvement with the world, rather than feeling like we need to step aside and let other people hold up the sky, giving up on the satisfaction of accomplishment and conscious engagement with the world.

Our ceilings and floors, our minimum and maximum capacities will change as our brains and bodies (and our extended components, like our relationships and work and assets) change. But we're capable of writing our own narratives, subbing-out those we're handed when we enter this world with more realistic, us-shaped tales that permit us to continue feeling as alive, worthy, and youthful (or as old, but in a good way) as we please.

Aging Rituals

The world's cultures are rich with coming-of-age ceremonies and rituals.

The South African Xhosa people's *ulwaluko* is a one-month initiation into adulthood for boys that begins with circumcision, involves seclusion and food (and sometimes water) restriction, and culminates with the burning of their childhood possessions, bathing in a river, and then returning to their communities as men.

In some Balian cultures, following a girl's first menstruation or a boy's voice initially breaking (in both cases signaling the arrival of puberty), the adults file down the teen's upper-canine teeth to symbolize the transition from the wild-animal world of childhood into their civilized, responsible, implicitly more human and less savage period of adulthood.

Some Asian cultures, like those in Japan and South Korea, have (or previously had) an annual "coming-of-age day" on which children who have recently reached the proper age (ranging from 15 to 20, depending on the local custom) are advised on their role as adults, are honored in some kind of ceremony, and often are dressed in some kind of ornamental costume.

Debuts or debutante balls are common in many parts of the world, and usually serve to both honor and celebrate a girl entering womanhood at the culturally appropriate age, but they also serve as an opportunity for would-be suitors to make themselves known, dance with the newly designated young woman, and possibly to present them with a gift.

Some such ceremonies mark the moment at which young people begin to learn a parent's (or some other community member's) trade, while others commemorate the adoption of another responsibility, like compulsory military service.

Almost all modern cultures have laws related to the age of a citizen, including those that affirm when they can learn to drive, purchase and consume alcohol or tobacco products, when they can vote, and whether they're of a legal age to consent to sex, marriage, or hired labor agreements.

These ceremonies, whatever their specifics, demarcate a transition from one stage of life into another, and one role (or collection of roles) within a society to another of the same.

As individuals pass through the entryway into adulthood, they often gain new benefits and rights, but are also burdened with additional responsibilities. Society almost always considers the shouldering of these roles to be an honor, celebrating an individual's transition into a fully realized member of the community, in contrast to their previous, often lesser positions as children.

The perceptual nature of all this is important, as a person can be a child one moment and an adult the next, in the eyes of society and the law. Which is fine for legal and ritualistic purposes, but it won't typically flag the actual moment at which that person crosses a threshold from immaturity into maturity—two highly subjective terms that are impossible to precisely and universally measure, to begin with.

That said, these rituals and celebrations provide a valuable means of partitioning moments of our lives, suggesting that one period is for being a borderline animal, responsible for nothing, another is for making sacrifices for our families and communities, and another, perhaps, is for relaxation and repose after all that dedication and hard work, during which we can enjoy the fruits of our (and our peers') labor, maybe even being revered for those earlier efforts.

There are global and historical examples of old-age rites of passage as well, but they are far fewer and less contemporarily well-practiced, in part because it wasn't until recently in human history that we've consistently lived past our 50s. Our youthful years also provide us with fairly (though not 100%) universal biological milestones around which to build such ceremonies, while our elder years do not.

Many woman will reach the end of their fertile period sometime between age 45 and 55, for instance, but this varies substantially, the timing and nature of what's often called menopause (or the climacteric) influenced by our genes, by habits like smoking and drinking, and by surgeries and treatments we have over the course of our lives.

It's possible to delineate and celebrate the transition from our baby-making years into whatever comes next, then, but it's not common in most cultures, and we're actually more likely to see the opposite: not a celebration of the transition from one way of being into another, but sadness or shame as we suffer from a flurry of new symptoms like bone deterioration, hot flashes, joint pain, and mood swings. There's also the vague sense that we're no longer at our peak, and that we are therefore less culturally (and romantically) relevant than before.

None of which is destiny, of course, and most of this age-associated vibe is a cultural response to normal biological realities, not a direct consequence of those realities.

Many aspects of puberty suck, after all, but we still manage to interpret that transition as something worth celebrating, so it stands to reason we could do the same with other life progressions as well, should we decide to do so.

At the moment, in the Western world in particular, the only real age-related celebrations many of us can expect in the second half of our lives are birthdays and maybe a retirement party. Even within the huge and growing array of fantastical, made-up holidays that keep greeting card companies in business, we find relatively few glorifications of post-reproductive age milestones (though there are plenty that playfully or earnestly mourn them).

A living funeral, though intuitively ghastly or somber, honors someone who is still with us, celebrating their lives and contributions, funeral-like, at a moment in which they can actually see the impact they've had on others, the beneficiaries of their time, attention, and wisdom celebrating that positive influence in their presence.

This sort of ceremony is typically held for someone who's terminally ill or very old, but it's imaginable that something similar—a middle-age celebration of life ceremony, or maybe one held for people in their 60s or 70s, regardless of their health circumstances—could become commonplace if enough of us hold them for our loved ones.

There's also a ceremony that was invented by a religious scholar in the 1980s called *simchat chochmah*, which celebrates a woman's transition from adulthood into elderhood, shifting from a period of bringing new life into the world and caring for that life, into an era defined by sharing her accumulated wisdom and providing mentorship to subsequent generations.

This ritual is based on other aging-focused religious celebrations, but rather than foregrounding the move from childhood into adulthood, it presents the elevation from adulthood into elderhood as honorable, necessary, and worthy, marking a moment at which someone who has lived and accomplished and sacrificed transcends their existing cares and considerations, continuing their journey of self-discovery in another context; thenceforth playing a different, but still valuable role in society.

There are other, more secular and often legally entangled rites we can expect to experience as we age, including (for some of us, at least) things like divorces, high school reunions, an ascension to the role of grandparent (or great-grandparent), and even moving into a retirement home or hospice care.

I like the idea of introducing new, innately celebratory and optimistic ceremonies for our twilight years, though, as significant portions of our lives are today culturally defined by what we've left behind; what we were, but are no longer.

That positions us as people who are failing at something we're no longer optimized for, rather than as people who are beginning our next adventure and growing into new versions of ourselves.

I value any opportunity to celebrate where we've been, what we've done, the hurdles we've leaped, and the iterations of ourselves we've flipped through on the way to becoming who we are today.

It can also be healthful to set aside time for mourning, for disconcertion, and to grieve so that we can address and move past these feelings, in the sense that they no longer dominate our thoughts, actions, and plans; so they don't define us, in our eyes, or in the eyes of others.

I think it would serve us, societally and individually, to introduce more such opportunities. Our lifespans (and healthspans) have increased dramatically in recent generations, so we have many more years to fill and hopefully enjoy, during which we'll ideally have more time to pause and reflect, smile at where we've been, and share what we've learned with younger generations, even as we confidently take the next step in our ongoing journeys.

Generational Transfer

Alongside tacit industry knowledge, which is often physical know-how, or quirks and specifics about dealing with particular vendors or clients, a large amount of institutional knowledge (everything all the people at a business or organization collectively know about work-related things) is stored only in the brains of employees.

Some institutions have tried to create internal wikis (systems that allow folks to share what they know in editable-by-anyone encyclopedias), but the benefits of these are mixed because they favor one type of encoding and sharing of information (writing it down), and because they often become ghost towns before they become useful enough for people to habituate referencing and adding to them.

The goal of these bits of (typically digital) infrastructure is to augment what's called institutional transfer: the communication of institutional knowledge between people working at a company or organization, enabling the communication of said knowledge between coworkers, but also between generations of workers.

That means not just making sure all the folks who currently work at a restaurant understand how the fiddly cookstove in the kitchen functions, but also ensuring that the next round of workers, and the next, and the next know how to turn the wonky knobs and which settings are optimal for which dishes.

Periodic kitchen staff turnover—everyone leaving at once, the knowledge they have about the stove and other kitchen peculiarities leaving with them—makes this sort of knowledge transmission difficult, as each new team is cursed with having to figure out how that stove works, burning or undercooking a lot of dishes in the meantime.

A similar issue, called "generational transfer," plagues humanity.

We've become skilled, as a species, at documenting and sharing things.

Unfortunately, while shared information is available somewhere, that doesn't mean most of us will ever reference it, know how to reference it if we wanted to, or will know said information is there to be referenced in the first place.

Imagine that restaurant launches its own internal wiki (containing information about the persnickety stove), but makes no announcement about it. The wiki exists, knowledge is ready to be soaked up by anyone who wants it, but because no one visits this resource, no one benefits from that investment and those recurring problems (which the wiki was meant to solve) persist.

In humanity's case, it's not that no one knows books, encyclopedias, and courses about many subjects exist, it's that we're overwhelmed by the deluge of other information, other media, and other entertainments, so the likelihood of us stumbling across a specific (perhaps vital) piece of knowledge is essentially zero.

We might know, intellectually, that we can learn just about anything for free on the internet, but we also know social media and cat videos are more fun, and they're typically less frictionful than the learny stuff, so we spent more of our time and attention on those.

There's also warranted concern about what's called the "digital dark age."

We live in an era of rapidly developing technologies and systems, so we adopt and retire communication mediums faster than previous generations.

This is good in the sense that newer mediums are typically better than older ones, but not so great because many of our earlier mediums, the ones we discarded in favor of the new ones, rapidly become inaccessible because we've moved on to the next set of standards.

The information contained on those disks, drives, tapes, file formats, and portions of the internet that are no longer used or usable, then, becomes inaccessible to almost everyone. That means huge portions of our species' cultural history go dark, buried in these now-antique mediums, almost like they never happened.

One consequence of such transitions is that we have trouble remembering, as a civilization, the lessons we learned during those less accessible periods.

Before we developed writing, we memorized and verbally communicated information, often in a narrative format to make that memorization and communication easier and more reliable; we transmitted valuable knowledge from person to person, and via the same means, generation to generation.

This helped us pass on wisdom, know-how, and historical understandings to other humans we would never meet: people who would live in very different worlds from our own, but who might still benefit from what we've learned, what we've lived through, and what we've picked up from earlier generations that left their own messages in temporal, verbally transmitted bottles.

It's through such channels that we've learned some of life's great lessons, and avoided having to relearn (at significant cost) others.

Intergenerational wisdom has even helped teach us about the value of intergenerational wisdom: after all, "Those who cannot remember the past are condemned to repeat it" (though other purveyors of topical wisdom claim history doesn't repeat itself, "it merely rhymes").

We have trouble trying to disseminate knowledge and understanding even between contemporaneous human peer-groups (those that live alongside each other), but this problem deepens as people age and die, and as new people arrive on the scene.

The totality of human comprehension and wisdom is continuously turning over, with a full Ship of Theseus-like reset every 70 or 80 years, at which point essentially everyone on the planet is new (measuring from that previous baseline).

It's up to us to decide what sort of mark we leave on the world and on those who will come after us, and it's the effort of each new generation to figure out how to encapsulate and communicate the fruits of our collective efforts to the holistic whole of humanity, contemporary and subsequent.

We benefit mightily from this continuum, this transfer of intellectual wealth, this huge-scale cross-pollination. But we also have the opportunity, the honor, maybe even (according to some ways of thinking, at least) the responsibility to add to it, to reinforce it, and to make it more accessible and valuable so those who come after us will make fewer of the mistakes we survived, and will start writing their own wikis, messages in bottles, and love letters from a loftier position of wisdom and knowledge than any generation that came before; our existence, our passage through life, our sharing of ourselves serving as raw materials for whatever they choose to build.

Mourning

It can be traumatic to lose our sense of self, or to detect a diminished connection with our brains, bodies, and lives; to feel estranged from previous iterations of our bodies, our connections to those bodies, and the connections our bodies had with the world; from our earlier states of mind, from the things we knew and how those things made us feel; from the relationships we had, from our hobbies, habits, rituals, and routines; from the things we cared about and prioritized—it all aggregates into a difficult sequence of transitions as we grow, change, and attempt to maintain our ties to the world as it changes around us.

However old we are, humans are prone to recalling mostly the good stuff, alongside a tempered version of the pointedly negative memories. But for most of us, our recollections of earlier years eventually come to seem superior to what we're experiencing now, and our (biological and cultural) child-rearing primes benefit most from this rosy retrospection, seeming—in our funhouse mirror recollections—to have been just stupidly amazing, and to have, thus, been the best days of our lives.

Note that we don't recall them this way because they objectively were the best days of our lives: as we lived through them, these periods were just as awash with discomforts, fears, pain, and every other element of the human condition as our current daily experience.

But it's in these moments, usually from our late-teens through our late-20s, that our senses are heightened, pop culture and marketing messaging revolve around us, and we often feel amazing, our muscles and minds working at more or less top capacity.

We thus long for these periods, but we're actually longing to feel the way we recall feeling in these eras, sans all the boring and not great stuff that we also lived through.

This romanticization of the past can influence absolutely everything about our present, shaping the choices we make, the things we prioritize, our relationships (with others, the world, and ourselves), and what we consider good, successful, and desirable.

This stance can cause internal strife and friction because we cannot be 20 again, not when we're already 40, just as we can't be 40 when we're 70.

It might be an appealing thought, the idea of revisiting those moments, feeling enlivened, heightened, and culturally central again, but it's not a realistic desire (not with today's technologies, at least).

But even if we do someday develop a therapy that allows us to reset our bodies and brain matter back to where they were decades earlier, structurally, that still wouldn't put us back in the shoes of our prior-selves, because the world that person lived in no longer exists, and the ignorant (compared to who we are now) perspective from which we viewed things at the time has been replaced by that of a wiser, more knowledgeable iteration of the same; we know and have experienced too much to be that person again.

The older we get, the more likely we are to have things to mourn, and the more time we're likely to spend mourning.

More people go away—moving, changing, dying—and more of our cherished ways of being, of living, of organizing our days and our plans dissipate as well.

We mourn the loss of our health, the breakups and divorces and the changes to friendships that over the years changed shape, becoming unrecognizable.

Our sense of youth, vitality, invincibly, and immortality go away, too, leaving us feeling very human, very meat-like, no longer the center of everything and thus scrambling for a sense of what it all means, why we're here, why like this, why why why.

We may try to imbue our suffering with meaning, but many of us discover that suffering often means nothing: it's like the weather, it just happens because of cascading, neutral, unthinking forces that are beyond our reckoning or control, and which are consequently difficult to incorporate into a personal hero's journey narrative.

The compounding elements of grief are more likely to hit us (like a chronological hammer) at some age-related milestones than others. But we face more blows the more years we accumulate, and many of these impacts will land without discernible rhyme, reason, or purpose.

Learning to mourn is fundamental to moving past these difficult moments. Although we won't always be able to claim a sense of significance as we suffer, we can face these trials productively if we give ourselves permission to fully experience and derive value from them.

Vital to accruing that value is coming to accept our personal transition from one state to another; one way of being to another.

We learn to mourn our lost hopes, dreams, intentions, and goals.

We learn to acknowledge minor or fundamental changes to "the way things are"—not by forgetting "the way things were," but by productively comparing and contrasting, allowing ourselves to become part of the new paradigm into which we've been thrust, and deciding to make the best of it, make it ours, just as we did with the previous one.

Acceptance is about recognizing and acknowledging loss without succumbing to (or drowning in) misery or depression. By allowing ourselves to experience this hollowness fully, and then filling it and ourselves with other things, we put ourselves on a path toward a new, healthful perceptual status quo.

Some problems are self-reinforcing, causing us to suffer way beyond the point that the pain teaches us anything useful. It's only by identifying and deciding to change how we respond to these problems that we stand any chance of halting that larger, negative cycle.

Mourning, accepting, and moving forward without denying or forgetting what came before is a muscle we can exercise and strengthen, making this process an easier lift (despite still being cumbersome) as we grow.

Afterword

Aging is one of the rare of activities we engage in from the moment we're born until the moment we die, every single moment of every single day defined, in part, by a process of cellular and cognitive iteration that's set in motion before we even leave the womb.

This process intertwines with every aspect of our lives, and if we approach it unintentionally, it can make us feel depleted and depreciated, rather than refined and ripened.

Thankfully, aging is something we can learn to do better, even if imperfectly, and by taking responsibility for it and rethinking our presumptions about what it means to be different ages, what it means to grow older, and what we're capable or incapable of at various stages of our lives, we're better prepared to face the eroding winds of times, to embrace our intrinsic and beautiful seasonality, and to make the absolute most of however many moments we're allotted.

Acknowledgments

Thanks to everyone who has ever taught me anything (basically every human with whom I've ever come into contact, and a lot more I've never met and will likely never meet).

Thanks to my family, and especially my parents, who have always been supportive of all the weird things I've decided to do with my life, and who continue to show me what it means to grow and mature with intent, rather than simply aging.

Thanks to my partner, Ariana, who's a brilliant artist and delightful person, and whose good-natured ribbing about my age helped inspire this book.

And thanks to you and everyone else who has supported my work over the years: I have a truly bizarre, me-shaped career, and this sort of model doesn't work without wonderful, interested, curious, enthusiastic people on the other end of the communications I optimistically hurl into the void. So thank you for keeping me company, thank you for supporting an independent maker-of-things, and thank you for empowering me to invest my time and energy in pursuits I wouldn't otherwise be able to justify.

About the Author

Colin Wright is a person who is learning in public. He just turned 39.

He travels a fair bit, juggles all sorts of projects and interests, and is fortunate to live a life filled with challenges, small victories, and wonderful people.

Visit colin.io to learn more about his books, podcasts, speaking engagements, and other such things.

Printed in Great Britain
by Amazon